Wild Weed Pie

Renowned chef Janni Kyritsis grew up in northern Greece, where he worked as an electrician and in the Greek merchant navy. Arriving in Melbourne in 1970 at the age of 24, he soon found a job as a 'sparkie' at the Melbourne Museum, and shortly after met his partner, David Bradshaw. David encouraged him to take up cooking as a way to learn English, and soon Janni became obsessed with all things culinary. The self-taught cook persuaded Stephanie Alexander to take him on at Stephanie's, where he stayed for 5 years, before moving to Sydney and Gay Bilson's internationally recognised Berowra Waters Inn in 1982. There the first *Sydney Morning Herald Good Food Guide* named Janni 1985 Chef of the Year, and the restaurant retained its three-hat status until it closed in 1995. Janni and Gay then moved to Sydney's iconic Bennelong in the Opera House.

Two years later, Janni opened his first restaurant, the multi-award-winning MG Garage, in partnership with Trivett Classic. MG Garage was awarded three chef's hats in its first year by the *Sydney Morning Herald Good Food Guide* and was also voted Best New Restaurant. In its second year, it was named Restaurant of the Year by the *Sydney Morning Herald Good Food Guide*, and thereafter picked up numerous other awards, such as *Gourmet Traveller*'s Best Restaurant of the Year, Restaurant and Catering's Best Restaurant in Australia, and Australian Gourmet Pages Restaurant of the Year. In 2002 Janni entered Restaurant and Catering's John K. Walker Hall of Fame for his contribution to the industry. In his career, Janni has been associated with 50 chef's hats from the *Sydney Morning Herald Good Food Guide*, more than any other chef. In 2002 he took a long break from full-time cooking, concentrating instead on his work for charities and on compiling recipes for this book. Janni lives in Sydney with David.

Wild Weed Pie

Janni Kyritsis

A lifetime of recipes

with Roberta Muir

Photography by Ian Wallace

LANTERN

an imprint of

PENGUIN BOOKS

Con

To David
my guardian,
my friend,
my lover,
for decades of encouragement,
of knowledge imparted,
and of guidance in every aspect of my life.

tents

Wild Weed Pie

Spring. Time to go on picnics in the fields. The oregano has come into flower and it has to be picked before it goes to seed and becomes bitter. 'Don't pick those little pink flowers,' Mother would say. 'They're wild oregano and are too strong' (she was actually talking about thyme).

I must have been about 6 or 7 when, on one of those family picnics, Mother showed me how to pick the most tender dandelion leaves. That night, as I watched the leaves being prepared, I was so pleased to have contributed to the family dinner – **Wild Weed Pie**.

Five women who influenced my career

Cooks often regard their mother's cooking as the main influence in their career, as do I. However, apart from my partner David's direction and guidance, I regard these five women as my main influence: Margaret Fulton, Stephanie Alexander, Gay Bilson, Josephine Pignolet and Duré Dara.

Margaret Fulton

Twenty-five years ago David thought it was a good idea that I learn English through an interest, and he gave me a Margaret Fulton cookbook. Thank you, Margaret.

In 1998 I was asked to make a comment on Margaret Fulton's then-latest cookbook. I was reminded of how I came to be a cook and gave this quote. I had become interested in cooking through watching David in the kitchen, and once I had Margaret's book I cooked and cooked from it and it gave me the start for my future career. It's not for me to tell the story of Margaret Fulton's contribution to Australian cooking, as everybody knows how great that has been. Years have passed, and today I regard Margaret not only as a teacher from all those years ago, but also as a good friend. I was very touched when, in a recent article, Margaret counted one of my dishes among those she would like to have for her last supper.

If you have limited time, forget about my recipes that require 2 days to make, forget the glossy cookbooks with their gastro-porn photography and recipes that can never be realised, and open the pages of one of Margaret's cookbooks.

Stephanie Alexander

If you are a dedicated cook – and a lot of Australians are – then Stephanie's *Cook's Companion* will already be on your kitchen bench, and if not, it ought to be.

After years of cooking, reading, becoming obsessed with everything about food, and walking around with an Elizabeth David paperback in the back pocket of my electrician's overalls for reading during any spare moments, it was time for me to change career. Stephanie had the foresight to allow a 30-year-old electrician into her kitchen, and for that I will always be grateful. She became my mentor and has remained so throughout my professional career.

From the first day I arrived at Stephanie's, I knew that this was what I wanted to do with my life, and I felt so lucky being there. Generosity is what I associate with Stephanie's food and her restaurant. There was always something extra on the plate, unexpected by the guests. Stephanie would go to great lengths to achieve this: minute leaves from the vegetable patch at the back of the restaurant; a scattering of chive flowers over a salad – details that weren't obvious but that made all the difference in her honest approach to cooking.

Hard work and dedication to the Australian food scene have rewarded Stephanie, who is now the Grande Dame of Australian cooking. Her timeless work, *The Cook's Companion*, sits very comfortably among the giants of cooking literature.

Gay Bilson

My introduction to Gay Bilson was through an article she wrote on making cakes. I was so taken by its clarity and straightforward explanations that I immediately thought I'd like to meet the person who wrote it. I later met Gay at the first Rothbury Estate Dinner in the Hunter Valley. Stephanie and I arrived there early from Melbourne to churn our sorbets, only to return at dinnertime to discover that they had melted because of a power failure. Gay, who was there to serve one of the courses, encouraged us not to give up but to start again – as we did. After a lot of exhausting work churning the sorbets by hand (which nobody does these days), we succeeded in serving them just on time.

From that introduction, I was convinced that if we ever moved to Sydney – as we later did – the only natural place for me to work would be with Gay at Berowra Waters Inn. I arrived there after Tony Bilson left, and there I learnt to pare my cooking down to the bare essentials and get to the heart of the ingredients. Gay loves books, art and architecture, and that was reflected in her restaurant and how it was run. She gave me the opportunity to be part of what became an iconic Australian restaurant with a philosophy of simplicity derived from years of experience and an understanding of the culinary arts. Gay and I went our separate ways in 1997 after 14 years of working together.

Josephine Pignolet

'Australia has lost perhaps its best cook.' So wrote Stephanie Alexander in Josephine's obituary in 1988, and I couldn't agree more.

This wonderful menu, cooked on my birthday in 1983 by Josephine and Damien Pignolet, would be just as relevant today as it was almost 25 years ago.

Salad of avocado with broad beans
Salmon caviar omelette
Boudin blanc on a spinach purée
Wild duck with turnips
Salade heureuse
Coffee and petits fours

Such timeless cooking is what I associate with Josephine. I first met her when she came to the old Stephanie's for a couple of days' work experience. She taught me how to cook brioche properly: how to prepare the knob in a cone shape to make sure it stays in the centre when it cooks. I can laugh now remembering my first attempts, before Josephine's lessons: I would make a long sausage-shaped roll of dough, cut it into 1 inch pieces and place them on top of the brioche balls – not exactly what a brioche should look like.

I used to help Josephine or Damien on Wednesdays at Claude's, so that one of them could have the night off. It was always a delight for me to be in that kitchen. When Josephine and Damien decided to put tomatoes on toast on the menu, it was a revelation to me. If you can find the perfect ingredients for a dish as simple as this, they should be left alone to speak for themselves. I have always tried to follow this philosophy in my own cooking.

I always remember a particularly funny incident with Josephine and Damien. One night, when Stephanie, David and I were having dinner at Claude's, David ordered the consommé under a puff-pastry lid. It looked spectacular when it arrived, but when David cracked the crust there was no consommé in the bowl! We laughed at the sight of the empty bowl, and so did the customers near us, but poor Josephine and Damien went red with embarrassment.

Duré Dara

I met Duré when she was managing front-of-house at Stephanie's. Because of her, I understand the importance of the front-of-house staff. A restaurant is about ambience, service and food. Certainly, if the food is not right, the customers won't come back, but it's these three elements together that make a restaurant. I observed Duré constantly, and little and unimportant incidents always taught me something about service.

I tried to impart this knowledge to the front-of-house staff at MG Garage and Fuel. Not that I ever needed to worry – with Colin Nelson at the helm I knew the customers were in good hands.

I remember one night a drunk old man walked into Stephanie's and sat at a table. Duré instantly handed her duties over to the rest of the staff and sat at the table with the old man. They talked for a bit, probably about the weather, but when he asked Duré for a drink, she said how sorry she was, but that we were a BYO restaurant. The old man left happy that somebody had talked to him, and all the other customers, who could see that the incident could have turned nasty, remained relaxed. Duré was always a step ahead, as if she could read the customers' minds. I was forever asking her questions about front-of-house, and I always received a sensible answer.

'This book would not have been written...'

This old line has never been truer than in this case. I couldn't have done it without my friend Roberta.

I first met Roberta Muir and Franz Scheurer when they came to MG Garage for a meal. They became our most regular customers and they had a good reason: they associated their romance with visits to our restaurant. Roberta got so enthusiastic about the food that she was constantly telling me I had to put together a book so that she could cook all her favourite dishes at home.

I never wanted to write a book. I still don't! I had contributed so many recipes over the years to other people's books and to magazines that I had no particular desire to write a book of my own. One day, Julie Gibbs at Penguin asked me to write a book, and from then on, if any other publisher asked me to write one, I'd say I'd already promised Julie. I repeated this line so often that in the end I believed it myself, but it was Roberta's persuasion that really convinced me. Poor girl, she had no idea how hard it would be to get into my dyslexic mind and extract every thought! But she did, and so this book is now written. And the first person I have to thank one more time is my dear friend Roberta.

Every chef will tell you that their best tool is their knife – and this is true. But ever since I first put my hand on a pasta machine years ago at Stephanie's, it has become an indispensable tool right throughout my career. I remember the first pasta I ever made, under Stephanie's instruction: beetroot noodles to go with venison. 'How bizarre and beautiful,' a food critic commented at the time. Berowra Waters saw a few pasta machines go to the scrapheap from overuse, as, for years, pasta was the staple for every table. But the reason I grew to love this little machine was the uses I got out of it apart from making pasta.

One day, while I was trying to make handmade Greek filo pastry, and becoming cross because I couldn't make it as thin as the women in my household traditionally did, I suddenly thought, 'How would it be if I passed it through the pasta machine?' Wow! What a discovery. I could now make my own thin sheets of filo – but not too thin, like commercial filo. The reason I prefer handmade filo to the commercial variety (which is, by the way, a fantastic product) is its texture – I like the bit of a bite that the handmade filo has. I find texture is very important in cooking; Chinese cuisine knows this very well, as does Italian, when it asks for pasta al dente.

But the little machine did not stop there. I used to make grissini by passing the bread or pizza dough through the thickest setting and either cutting it into shapes by hand, or passing it through the fettucine-cutter to get uniformly thin grissini. I also passed bread dough through on the thickest setting to make flatbread, or on the finest setting to make thin crackers, which I glazed with egg white and sprinkled liberally with sesame seeds before baking. Cutting 5 cm wide strips and baking or deep-frying them makes wonderful biscuits for an appetiser. In the same way I've made crostoli by passing pastry dough through the machine, twisting and deep-frying it and dousing it in plenty of icing sugar. Cutting large discs, rolling them loosely around wooden dowels (the thickness of a broomstick) and deep-frying them gives cannoli or thinner 'cigarettes' to fill with sweet or savoury creams. I also use the machine to roll Scandinavian crisp rye bread (see page 22). And lastly, if you need to make your own Chinese pancakes for Peking duck, the pasta machine will give you very good, evenly sized discs.

anchovies deep-fried in gremolata breadcrumbs with green tartare sauce

Makes 12

12 anchovy fillets, drained (see page 172)
¼ cup plain flour
1 egg, lightly beaten
1 cup Gremolata Breadcrumbs
　　(see page 175)
olive oil, for deep-frying

Green tartare sauce

50 g baby spinach
1 egg yolk
1 teaspoon Dijon mustard
2 teaspoons strained lemon juice
salt, to taste
freshly ground black pepper, to taste
150 ml light olive oil
¼ cup finely sliced cornichons
　　(see page 172)
1½ tablespoons small salted capers,
　　blanched (see page 174)
2 tablespoons chopped flat-leaf
　　parsley leaves
1 tablespoon snipped chives
2 teaspoons chopped French
　　tarragon leaves
2 golden shallots, finely chopped
1 hard-boiled egg, finely chopped

Anchovies are one of my favourite flavours, and make a very good starter; the saltiness and piquancy make my mouth water. I love this appetiser so much I could eat it as an entrée with some salad and plenty of green tartare sauce. I find traditional tartare sauce a bit rich with fish and chips, so I always use this lighter, green version. The herbs you use in the sauce can vary with the season and your imagination.

To make the green tartare sauce, wash the spinach and, with water still clinging to the leaves, place in a saucepan over medium heat and cook for a few seconds until wilted. Squeeze well to remove excess liquid, then chop finely. Place egg yolk, mustard, lemon juice, salt and pepper in a small bowl and whisk well to combine. Continuing to whisk, slowly add the olive oil, drop by drop at first, then in a slow, steady stream, until all the oil is incorporated and a mayonnaise has formed. Thoroughly mix the cornichons, capers, parsley, chives, tarragon and shallots into the spinach. Fold the spinach mixture into the mayonnaise and mix well. Gently fold in the chopped egg. Cover and refrigerate.

　　Dip anchovies in flour, then egg, then Gremolata Breadcrumbs, pressing the bread-crumbs firmly onto the anchovies. Dip in egg again, then again in the Gremolata Breadcrumbs, leaving this second coating loose. Heat the olive oil in a frying pan and deep-fry the anchovies until golden. Serve the green tartare sauce separately.

Braised herb-stuffed globe artichokes

Serves 8

juice of 1 lemon, strained
8 large globe artichokes
1 cup extra-virgin olive oil
1 large brown onion, finely chopped
6 teaspoons chopped thyme leaves
2 teaspoons chopped dill
½ cup chopped flat-leaf parsley leaves
1 medium carrot, thinly sliced
8 cloves garlic, peeled
grated zest of 1 lemon
1 cup dry white wine
salt, to taste
freshly ground black pepper, to taste
1 kg fresh broad beans
8 slices sourdough baguette
extra-virgin olive oil, extra, for brushing
8 cloves garlic, extra, very thinly sliced
    and blanched (see page 174)
zest of ½ lemon, extra, blanched (see
    page 174) and cut into thin strips
¼ cup flat-leaf parsley leaves, extra,
    very roughly chopped

✱ Turn these artichokes into a delicious salad by quartering and mixing with young rocket and crisp pancetta. Use some of the pan juices as a dressing.

My friend Maggie Beer once told me my artichoke dish at MG Garage was the best she'd ever tasted. The artichokes themselves taste even better the next day.

Add the lemon juice to a bowl of water large enough to hold the prepared artichokes. Artichokes discolour very quickly once cut, so prepare one artichoke at a time and keep them in the lemon water. Aluminium also makes artichokes discolour, so it's important not to use aluminium pans or utensils when cooking them. Trim the stem of the first artichoke, leaving 5 cm attached. Snap off outer leaves until tender leaves with a green–yellow base appear. Cut off the top third to remove the remaining coarse leaf tops. Peel the remaining stem, cut the artichoke in half lengthwise and, using a teaspoon, scoop out and discard the hairy choke from the centre. Immerse in the lemon water while you prepare the other artichokes.

Heat 100 ml of the olive oil in a large frying pan that has a lid, add the well-drained artichokes and fry for a few minutes, until golden, in batches if necessary (if you crowd the pan, they'll stew instead of fry). Remove from pan and set aside. Heat remaining olive oil in the same pan then add onion and fry until golden. Allow onion to cool then add chopped herbs.

Pack the onion and herb mixture into the centre of each artichoke and between the leaves. Return stuffed artichokes to the frying pan in a single layer, cut-side up. Arrange carrot, garlic and lemon zest around the artichokes. Pour in wine and sprinkle over salt and pepper. Cover with dampened baking paper and a lid then simmer over low heat for 20–30 minutes, until soft at fleshy base. Allow to cool to room temperature.

Meanwhile, preheat oven to 200°C. Prepare broad beans by removing them from their pods and blanching in boiling water for 30 seconds (see page 174). Run under cold water then remove from skins; you should end up with about 1 cup green broad beans. Toss them in a tablespoon of the cooking liquid and set aside.

Brush bread slices with olive oil. Bake on a baking sheet until golden, about 10 minutes.

Arrange 2 artichoke halves on a slice of bread, with a clove of garlic, some carrot slices and some cooking liquid, and garnish with broad beans, garlic slices, strips of lemon zest and extra parsley.

Parmesan cheese wafers with parmesan cream, pear + apple balsamic

Serves 6
200 g parmesan cheese (see page 172),
    coarsely grated
3 ripe Corella pears
1½ tablespoons apple balsamic vinegar

Parmesan cream
150 ml milk
150 g finely grated parmesan cheese
1 cup 45%-fat cream

✱ The wafers will keep for up to a week in an airtight container with kitchen paper between the layers, and can be recrisped in the oven for a minute if they've become a bit soft.

At MG Garage I often served this as part of the cheese course, sometimes making gruyère wafers instead of parmesan (but always with parmesan cream). You can also use apples or other pears, such as Williams, in this recipe. Balsamic vinegar can be used instead of apple balsamic vinegar, or you can make your own by grating a green apple, combining it with a cup of good balsamic vinegar, bringing it to the boil, straining, then reducing the liquid by half; cool before use.

To make the parmesan cream, combine milk and cheese in a small saucepan and, stirring constantly, heat until melted, just before boiling. Strain immediately and allow to cool. Fold in cream and whisk until thick. Refrigerate until required.

Preheat oven to 165°C. To make parmesan wafers, sprinkle the cheese into 18 circles on a non-stick baking tray, using an egg ring or an 8 cm biscuit cutter as a guide. Bake for 7–8 minutes or until golden. If they are too pale they'll be chewy, and if too brown they'll be bitter, so watch them closely. Remove from tray while still warm, using a spatula. Cool on a wire rack and store in an airtight container with kitchen paper between the layers.✱

Just before serving, quarter and core pears then slice thinly. To serve, place a dab of parmesan cream on each plate to hold wafer in place. Top with a wafer, a few slices of pear, 1 teaspoon parmesan cream and a drizzle of balsamic vinegar. Repeat layering once more, finishing with a third wafer.

Mushroom, spinach + ricotta pasta roll with caper butter

Serves 6

¼ cup extra-virgin olive oil
1 clove garlic, chopped
400 g large mushrooms, sliced
½ teaspoon ground coriander seeds
salt, to taste
freshly ground black pepper, to taste
30 g butter
1 medium red onion, finely chopped
pinch freshly grated nutmeg
2 teaspoons chopped thyme leaves
60 g parmesan cheese (see page 172), grated
800 g baby spinach leaves
200 g ricotta
kitchen twine
125 g butter, extra
2 tablespoons small salted capers, blanched (see page 174)
100 g parmesan cheese, extra, shaved

Fresh pasta

2 eggs
5 egg yolks
1 tablespoon olive oil
350 g plain flour, sifted
large pinch salt

✱ The roll can be kept in the refrigerator for a few hours before poaching; add an extra 5 minutes to the cooking time.

For many years I made a pasta roll with tomato sauce from a recipe in Marcella Hazan's *Classic Italian Cookbook*. Then I discovered a more refined version in Rose Gray and Ruth Roger's wonderful *River Café Cook Book*, which inspired this particular recipe.

To make the pasta, beat eggs and yolks together lightly with the olive oil. Sift flour and salt into a mound on a clean, dry work surface. Make a well in the centre of the mound, pour in egg mixture and, using a fork, incorporate the flour into the egg mixture. Knead until smooth, roll into a ball, wrap in plastic film and leave to sit at room temperature for 30 minutes.

Meanwhile, heat oil in a frying pan, add garlic and mushrooms and cook over a high heat for a couple of minutes until most of the liquid has evaporated. Add ground coriander, salt and pepper, and set aside to cool. Melt the 30 g butter in a frying pan and fry onion until golden. Mix in nutmeg, thyme, grated parmesan, salt and pepper. Tip into a mixing bowl and set aside to cool. Wash spinach leaves and, with water still clinging to them, place them in the same pan and cook over high heat until wilted. Tip into a colander and run over cold water for a moment to cool them down. Drain well, squeeze to remove excess water and chop roughly. Fold spinach into onion mixture and set aside to cool.

Unwrap dough, cut into 3 pieces, dust with flour and pass each piece through a pasta machine about 10 times until smooth and no longer sticky, sprinkling with extra flour as needed. Once smooth, continue to pass the pasta through the machine, reducing the setting each time until you reach the third-last setting.

Place a clean, colourfast tea towel on a work surface. Place pasta sheets on the tea towel side by side, overlapping slightly, to form a 30 cm square. Rub a little water along the joins and press gently to seal.

Spread mushroom mixture on half the square, and spinach mixture on the other half, leaving a border all around of about 2 cm. Arrange chunks of ricotta on top of the spinach. Using the tea towel to guide the pasta, roll it up like a Swiss roll. Wrap the roll in the tea towel and tie securely with kitchen twine.✱ Bring a large pan (a fish kettle is ideal) of salted water to the boil, reduce heat to a simmer and poach roll, in the tea towel, for 20 minutes.

Just before serving, heat the extra 125 g butter in a frying pan until it starts to colour. Add capers and fry for a few seconds then remove from heat. Unwrap roll, cut into slices and serve with caper butter and parmesan shavings.

Garlic soup with poached egg + parmesan

Serves 6

250 g peeled garlic cloves
1 cup light olive oil
1 litre Chicken Stock* (see page 176)
1 tablespoon thyme leaves,
    tied securely in muslin
3 teaspoons salt
2 teaspoons freshly ground white pepper
2 tablespoons Fresh Breadcrumbs
    (see page 175)
2 tablespoons strained lemon juice
6 slices sourdough baguette
6 eggs
parmesan cheese, shaved, to garnish

* This soup is equally good when made with a light Fish Stock or Vegetable Stock (see pages 175 and 177).

I love garlic. As a child I was told to eat plenty, so I wouldn't get a cold. But today I love garlic for its flavour rather than its medicinal value. Almost every cuisine in the world places garlic among its prized ingredients, except for those of English-speaking countries. One of my most loved dishes comes from French cuisine: a chicken is roasted with 40 cloves of garlic in their skins, and then the soft purée is extracted to make a sauce. This simple garlic soup is one of the best I ever made and, to my surprise, it was very popular at MG Garage. Maybe it was its simplicity, maybe some customers liked it and told their friends. I don't know. You'll need about 4 heads garlic for this recipe.

Place garlic cloves in a small saucepan with the olive oil. Bring to the boil, reduce heat to very low, cover and simmer for about 20 minutes, until very soft. Take care not to burn the garlic or it will become bitter. Add the stock and thyme, bring to the boil, then reduce heat and simmer for a further 15 minutes. Strain and retain stock, reserving garlic cloves and discarding thyme. Add salt and pepper to the stock. Cool, then skim off and retain the oil from the surface.

Preheat oven to 150°C. Purée the reserved garlic cloves with the breadcrumbs, lemon juice and half the reserved oil from the stock. Taste and add extra salt and pepper if necessary. Add half the purée to the stock and mix well. Check seasoning again.

Brush bread slices with the remaining oil from the stock and bake for about 10 minutes, until golden. Spread with the remaining garlic purée.

Three-quarters fill a large frying pan with water. Bring to the boil, then reduce heat to a simmer. Break in the eggs and poach for 2–3 minutes.

Place a bread slice in each soup bowl, top with an egg, then gently pour over soup and garnish with parmesan shavings.

Red capsicum + eggplant roll with black olive + thyme focaccia

Serves 6

2 large eggplants
salt, to purge eggplants
6 large red capsicums
olive oil, for shallow-frying
1 tablespoon balsamic vinegar
3 tablespoons extra-virgin olive oil
2 tablespoons chopped chives
½ cup chopped flat-leaf parsley leaves
salt, to taste
freshly ground black pepper, to taste
extra-virgin olive oil, extra, for serving

Black olive & thyme focaccia

7 g dry yeast (1 sachet)
¾ cup warm water
450 g baker's flour
1 teaspoon salt
⅓ cup dry white wine
⅓ cup extra-virgin olive oil
150 g pitted black niçoise or Ligurian olives
½ tablespoon chopped thyme leaves
extra-virgin olive oil, extra, for brushing

I first tasted a terrine of eggplant and capsicum at a lunch at Joan Campbell's, cooked by her daughter, Sue Fairlie-Cuninghame. Gay Bilson was very taken by the terrine, so I decided to create a roulade using the same ingredients – and this dish was born. The focaccia recipe is adapted from one in Claudia Roden's *Food of Italy*.

To make the focaccia, mix yeast with warm water in a small bowl and leave for 5 minutes. Combine flour and salt in a large bowl, make a well in the centre and pour in the yeast mixture. Using a fork, pull flour into water and mix until dry and crumbly. Add white wine and olive oil and mix until combined. Tip onto a clean, dry, floured surface and knead for 5 minutes, or until smooth. Return dough to mixing bowl, cover with plastic film and leave in a warm place for 2 hours, or until doubled in size. Place dough on a clean, dry, floured surface and spread into a 1 cm thick rectangle. Sprinkle olives and thyme over half the dough, fold the other half over to enclose, and pat down firmly, leaving no air pockets.

Place dough on an oiled baking tray, cover very loosely with plastic film, and leave for 30 minutes to 1 hour, until doubled in size. Preheat oven to 175°C. Remove plastic film, dimple top of dough with fingers, brush liberally with extra-virgin olive oil and bake for 20–30 minutes, until golden. Leave to cool on a wire rack.

Increase oven temperature to 220°C. Slice the eggplant lengthwise as thinly as possible (a mandoline is ideal – see page 173). Sprinkle with salt and leave to drain for 30 minutes. Brush capsicums with a little olive oil and roast in oven until skin blackens, turning carefully to ensure they blacken all over. I prefer to roast capsicums in the oven, as it also cooks the capsicums, improving their flavour and texture. Place roasted capsicums in a plastic bag until cool enough to handle, then remove the core, open out and remove any remaining seeds and membrane. Peel off and discard skin and pat flesh dry with kitchen paper (do not wash, as this removes flavour). Heat oil in a frying pan. Wipe eggplant slices dry and shallow-fry on both sides until pale brown. Drain on kitchen paper.

Lay sheets of plastic film on a damp bench to form a 50 cm square, overlapping them slightly so they hold together. Top with another layer of plastic film. Arrange eggplant slices on top, in a 40 × 30 cm rectangle, leaving no gaps. Lay the capsicum over the eggplant. Drizzle over the balsamic vinegar and extra-virgin olive oil and sprinkle over chopped chives, parsley, salt and pepper. With the aid of the plastic film, roll up into a roll of 6 cm diameter. Wrap tightly in the plastic film, tie ends and chill for a few hours or overnight.

Slice roll, through plastic film, into 6 rounds 4 cm thick. Cut 6 thick slices of focaccia, brush liberally with extra olive oil and toast lightly on a baking tray. Place a round on each plate and remove plastic film. Drizzle over lots of extra olive oil and serve with focaccia.

Olives, garlic + tomato in handmade filo pastry with anchovy sauce

Serves 6

24 Kalamata olives, pitted*
extra-virgin olive oil, to cover
24 cloves garlic, peeled
6 × 30 cm sheets Greek Filo Pastry
    (see page 177)
100 g butter, melted
½ cup roughly chopped black olives
2 witlof heads, each cut lengthwise into
    6 slices
3 tomatoes, blanched (see page 174),
    peeled and cut into 4 slices each

Anchovy sauce

65 g drained anchovy fillets
    (see page 172)
1 clove garlic
5 teaspoons strained lemon juice
pinch white pepper
100 ml extra-virgin olive oil

✳ To remove olive flesh from the stones, place olives between 2 tea towels and hit them gently with the palm of your hand or a meat mallet.

We held quite a few special dinners at MG Garage, including the 'Hats Off' dinners for the *Sydney Morning Herald* Good Food Month. One close to my heart was called 'Under the Greek Influence'. That dinner was a turning point for me because it was the first time I looked back to my roots for inspiration. Before then I'd never thought about how much my Greek heritage had influenced my cooking. I'm inspired by the poem 'Ithaca' by K. Kavafis (in turn inspired by Homer's *Odyssey*), which reminds me that I embarked upon a culinary journey around the world only to arrive back at the flavours I love most. I first developed this dish for the 'Greek Influence' dinner. It uses traditional filo pastry, made by hand, an art that has been largely lost since the introduction of commercial filo. Using a small pasta machine to roll the pastry means making your own filo is perfectly possible.

Put olives in a small saucepan and add enough olive oil to just cover. Bring just to the boil, reduce heat to very low, then cover and simmer for about 30 minutes, or until olives have lost most of their acidity and have a rich olive oil flavour.

Place garlic cloves in another small saucepan and add enough olive oil to just cover. Bring to the boil, reduce heat to very low, then cover and simmer for about 30 minutes, or until the garlic is very soft and no longer tastes raw. However, take care not to burn the garlic, or it will become bitter. Set aside and keep warm.

While the olives and garlic are cooking, make the anchovy sauce. Combine anchovies, garlic, lemon juice and pepper in a blender until smooth. With motor still running, slowly add the oil. The sauce should have a pouring consistency; add warm water to thin it down if necessary.

Preheat oven to 175°C. Place 1 sheet of filo pastry on a buttered baking tray. Brush with melted butter and sprinkle with chopped olives. Place a second sheet of filo pastry on top, pat down gently, and brush with butter. Cut assembled filo layers in half lengthwise, then cut crosswise into 6 squares. Repeat with remaining filo, butter and chopped olives on more baking trays. Bake for 6–8 minutes, until golden.

Place a filo square on each plate, then add layers of 2 garlic cloves, 2 olives, 1 witlof slice, 1 tomato slice and 1 teaspoon anchovy sauce. Top with a second filo square, repeat layers and finish with a third filo square.

Fassolada (baked lima bean soup) + pickles

Serves 6

½ cup extra-virgin olive oil
2 medium brown onions, chopped into
    1 cm dice
150 g baby carrots, sliced on the diagonal
1 small stick celery, sliced on the diagonal
½ green capsicum, chopped into 1 cm dice
3 cloves garlic, finely chopped
1 kg tomatoes, blanched (see page 174),
    peeled and seeded, juices reserved and
    strained, flesh chopped into 1 cm dice
1 tablespoon tomato paste
½ cup water
300 g dried lima beans, soaked overnight,
    drained and peeled
pinch ground cinnamon
pinch ground cloves
½ teaspoon dried Greek oregano
    (see page 172)
salt, to taste
freshly ground black pepper, to taste
2 tablespoons roughly chopped flat-leaf
    parsley leaves, to serve
extra-virgin olive oil, extra, to serve
olives, to serve
pickled vegetables,* to serve (optional)

* Greek pickled vegetables are available in
Greek delicatessens. Bear in mind if adding
more water that this soup is traditionally
served as a main course and so is quite
thick. Dried beans vary enormously
in their cooking times, depending on
their age, so you may need to adjust
accordingly.

In Greece when I was young, lima beans were often baked in big ovens
at the local bakery and devoured for lunch. Water would be added to the
remainder in the evening to make a soup, often served with olives and other
pickled vegetables (such as onion, cabbage, cauliflower and chillies) on the
side. In this recipe I have combined both of these ideas.

Preheat oven to 170°C. Heat oil in a large, heavy-based casserole dish and cook onions,
carrots, celery, capsicum and garlic over medium heat for 6–8 minutes or until soft but
not browned. Add tomatoes, reserved juice, tomato paste and water, and bring to the
boil. Add beans and stir well, then cover and transfer to oven for 1 hour or until beans
are tender. Add a little extra water during cooking if necessary.* Gently stir in cinnamon,
cloves and oregano, season to taste and cook for another 10–15 minutes or until beans
are very tender and almost falling apart.* Do not stir again.

    Sprinkle over parsley, drizzle over extra olive oil and serve from the casserole dish.
Pass olives and pickles separately, if desired.

Risotto balls with baked green tomatoes

Serves 6

2 tablespoons extra-virgin olive oil
2 tablespoons butter
1 small brown onion, chopped
250 g arborio rice
1 litre hot Chicken Stock (see page 176)
30 g grated parmesan cheese (see page 172)
1 egg
salt, to taste
freshly ground white pepper, to taste
20 g dried porcini mushrooms,
     soaked in warm water until soft
     (about 30 minutes)
150 g fontina cheese, cut into 12 cubes
2 cups Fresh Breadcrumbs (see page 175)
vegetable oil, for deep-frying

Baked green tomatoes

½ kg green tomatoes,* sliced
5 large golden shallots, sliced
2 cloves garlic, sliced
2 dried bay leaves, crushed
salt, to taste
freshly ground black pepper, to taste
½ cup dry white wine
¼ cup extra-virgin olive oil

✱ Green tomatoes can't be peeled easily by blanching, but as they are quite firm, they are easy to peel using a vegetable peeler. If you want to make a classic risotto, follow the first part of the recipe; when the rice is just cooked (al dente) and still moist, stir in a generous knob of butter and some grated parmesan.

A risotto, as I understand it, consists of perfectly cooked grains surrounded by their sauce – the secret lies in the type of rice used and in the constant stirring. For the tenth anniversary of Berowra Waters Inn, Gay Bilson thought it would be lovely to serve each guest a bowl of risotto. I jumped at the challenge and, after weeks of experimenting with timing, serving endless risottos at staff dinners, the kitchen team finally worked out the logistics of serving 400 people a dish that is normally cooked to order. It required 9 portable gas burners and 16 pans, each holding 25 serves. With a pan going out about every 2 minutes, in half an hour each of the 400 guests had been served their perfectly cooked mussel risotto. Don't be afraid to enlist the help of your friends and try serving risotto at your next garden party! Traditionally, risotto balls are made as a way to use up a family's leftover risotto. Ham, cheese and vegetables are all good additions.

Preheat oven to 175°C. To make the baked green tomatoes, peel the tomatoes with a vegetable peeler or paring knife* and cut into thick slices. Arrange shallots, garlic and bay leaves in a non-aluminium baking dish. Layer tomatoes on top, sprinkle with salt and pepper, and pour over white wine and olive oil. Bake for 30 minutes or until most of the liquid has evaporated, basting regularly with the juices.

To make the risotto, heat the olive oil and half the butter in a large saucepan, then add the onion and fry until golden. Add the rice and stir to coat well. Add a ladleful of hot stock and stir until almost all is absorbed. Continue adding the stock a ladleful at a time, stirring constantly and allowing each ladleful to be absorbed before adding the next. It will take about 20 minutes for the risotto to cook. If you run out of stock, use hot water.*

To make the risotto balls, keep cooking the risotto until it's very dry. Remove from heat, allow to cool, then stir in the parmesan, egg and salt and pepper. Mix well and set aside. Drain the porcini, squeeze dry and chop roughly. Melt remaining butter in a small pan and cook porcini for 1 minute. Season with salt and pepper and set aside. Divide risotto into 12 portions. Line the palm of your hand with plastic film, then spread a portion of risotto over the plastic film. Place 1 teaspoon porcini mushrooms and 1 cube fontina in the centre of the risotto. With the help of the plastic film, surround the porcini and fontina with the risotto, making sure they're well covered. Unwrap the balls carefully then gently roll them in breadcrumbs. Deep-fry balls until golden and serve with baked green tomatoes.

Escabeche of red mullet with broad-bean cake + broad bean, cucumber + preserved lemon salad

Serves 6

500 g red mullet fillets, bones removed
salt, to taste
plain flour, to coat fish
1 cup extra-virgin olive oil
1 medium brown onion, sliced
3 cloves garlic, skin on
150 ml red wine vinegar
2 sprigs thyme
2 dried bay leaves
1 bird's-eye chilli, sliced
extra-virgin olive oil, extra, for serving

Broad-bean cake

250 g dried broad beans, soaked overnight
    in plenty of water
1½ tablespoons extra-virgin olive oil
1 medium brown onion, finely chopped
3 cloves garlic, chopped
2 cups water
1 teaspoon dried Greek oregano
    (see page 172)
½ teaspoon salt
½ teaspoon freshly ground black pepper

Broad bean, cucumber & preserved lemon salad

1 kg fresh broad beans
12 slices Preserved Lemons (see page 178)
2 Lebanese cucumbers, peeled, halved
    and seeded
salt flakes, to taste
freshly ground black pepper, to taste
6 mint leaves, chopped
squeeze lemon juice
extra-virgin olive oil, to taste

✱ Cooking times for dried beans vary
enormously: some will cook in just 1 hour,
whereas others will take up to 3 hours.

During Lent, devout Greeks abstain from eating any animal products for 40 days, so many good vegetarian dishes are popular at this time. I remember a Lenten dish from my childhood of a broad-bean cake served cold and coated liberally with olive oil – not an appetising sight or taste for a child. I don't have the traditional recipe, but I've created this version from my mental image of that dish from so many years ago. Now I'm an adult, I can see what my parents saw in it. If you don't have time to make my Preserved Lemons for this recipe, you can use some blanched lemon zest cut into fine strips. Don't use other preserved lemons for this dish.

To make the broad-bean cake, drain, peel and split the dried broad beans. Heat olive oil in a large saucepan and fry onions and garlic until golden. Add broad beans and water, cover tightly and cook over a very low heat for 2–3 hours,✱ until beans are extremely soft, checking from time to time to see if more water is required. Uncover, increase heat and, stirring constantly with a wooden spoon, cook until you can make a mound of the mixture in the centre of the pot and the wooden spoon will just stand up in the middle of the mound. Add oregano and salt and pepper. Pour onto a baking tray lined with plastic film and spread into a rectangle 2 cm thick. Refrigerate to set.

To make the escabeche, sprinkle fish lightly with salt and coat lightly in flour. Heat half the 1 cup olive oil in a frying pan and fry the fillets for a couple of minutes until lightly browned. Place on a tray and set aside. Heat the remaining ½ cup oil in a large frying pan, then add the onion and garlic and fry until onion is golden brown. Add the remaining ingredients and cook over a high heat for a few minutes until most of the vinegar has evaporated. Pour the mixture over the fish and leave to marinate for a couple of hours at room temperature.

Meanwhile, make the salad. Remove broad beans from their pods and blanch (see page 174) in boiling water for 30 seconds. Run under cold water, then remove skins; you should end up with about 1 cup green broad beans. Cut each preserved lemon slice into quarters. Slice cucumbers finely. Combine all ingredients.

Preheat oven to 250°C. Remove garlic, bay leaves and thyme from the escabeche and discard. Carefully cut broad bean cake into 6 pieces (it can crumble easily, so you will need to be very careful). Place on an oiled non-stick baking tray and bake for a few minutes, until lightly browned. Carefully place a piece of broad bean cake on each plate, drizzle over extra olive oil and share the salad among the plates. Place the escabeche (including the onions and chilli) beside the salad.

Oysters with leeks in lemon butter

1 leek, white part only
50 g salted butter
salt, to taste
freshly ground white pepper, to taste
½ cup vegetable oil, for frying
2½ tablespoons strained lemon juice
2 teaspoons 35%-fat cream
250 g cold salted butter, cubed
6 oysters, opened

✱ Leftover leek mixture is delicious with fish. To use leftover cold lemon butter: heat 1 tablespoon cream in a saucepan and whisk in pieces of lemon butter; serve over any steamed or pan-fried fish.

Preheat oven to 220°C. Discard tough outer leaves of leek, slice in half lengthwise, trim off root and wash thoroughly under running water to get rid of any sand. Cut off 5 cm at the root ends and cut into very fine strips for a garnish. Slice remainder of leek. Melt butter in a small saucepan, add sliced leek and cook over a low heat until the leek is very soft and seems to have 'melted'. Add salt and pepper and set aside.

Heat vegetable oil in a small saucepan and deep-fry thin strips of leek garnish until crisp. Drain well on kitchen paper and set aside. Heat lemon juice in a small saucepan and boil until reduced to 2 teaspoons. Reduce heat to low and mix in cream. Whisk butter, piece by piece, into the lemon and cream mixture, ensuring the sauce doesn't get too hot, or it will separate.

Remove oysters from shells. Place 1 heaped teaspoon of the leek mixture in each shell and heat in oven for a couple of minutes. Place oysters on top and return to oven for 1 more minute. Add 1 teaspoon lemon butter and garnish with a few wisps of fried leek.

Oysters with laver bread & bacon

30 g dried wakame seaweed, soaked in
    hot water for 1 hour
½ cup vegetable oil
1 medium brown onion, chopped
1½ tablespoons soy sauce, or to taste
2 teaspoons hot English mustard, or
    to taste
1 tablespoon butter
1 rasher rindless bacon, cut into thin strips
6 oysters, opened

✱ Leftover seaweed mixture can be used as a garnish for fish. Wakame seaweed is available in Asian grocery shops with Japanese sections.

The first time I heard the term 'laver bread' was on a tape of Dylan Thomas narrating *Quite Early One Morning*: 'I was a stranger to the sea town, fresh or stale from the city where I worked for my bread and butter wishing it were laver-bread.' That sparked my interest, and I found out, from Jane Grigson's *Vegetable Book*, that laver is a seaweed from the Welsh coast. After having tasted laver bread brought to me by a Welsh friend, I tried to match the flavour using wakame seaweed. Although a Welshman might question how well I've succeeded in recreating the flavour, I think it's quite close, and I can't think of a more suitable name for this recipe.

Drain and chop seaweed very finely, discarding very tough stems. Heat oil in a small saucepan and cook onion over a low heat until very soft. Add seaweed and cook over a very low heat for almost 1 hour, until it looks oily rather than watery and is very soft. Season with soy sauce and mustard. Set aside.

Heat butter in a non-stick frying pan, add bacon and fry until crisp. Set aside for garnish.

Preheat oven to 220°C. Remove oysters from shells. Place 1 heaped teaspoon seaweed mixture in each shell and heat in oven for a couple of minutes. Place oysters on top and return to oven for 1 more minute. Garnish with crisp bacon and serve.

Oysters Rockefeller

75 g butter
5 cm piece celery, chopped
2 spring onions, sliced
¼ cup chopped flat-leaf parsley leaves
2 teaspoons chopped French tarragon
   leaves
200 g baby spinach leaves, washed and
   squeezed dry
3 teaspoons Pernod
4 drops Tabasco sauce, or to taste
salt, to taste
½ cup Fresh Breadcrumbs (see page 175)
6 oysters

According to Peter S. Feibleman's *American Cooking: Creole and Acadian*, Oysters Rockefeller was created in the late 1800s in Antoine's Restaurant in New Orleans. The story goes that it was called Rockefeller, after oil millionaire John D. Rockefeller, because the sauce was so rich.

Heat butter in a frying pan and cook celery and spring onions until soft. Add parsley, tarragon and spinach, and cook until most of the water has evaporated, 5–10 minutes. Add Pernod, Tabasco sauce, salt, and enough breadcrumbs to make a thick purée (you may not need all the breadcrumbs, depending on how dry the spinach mixture is). Purée in a blender or food processor until smooth; if it seems too liquid, add more breadcrumbs. It needs to be so dry that you have to scrape the sides of the blender regularly with a spatula, to keep the mixture moving. Check seasoning and add extra Tabasco or salt if required. Refrigerate until cold.

Preheat oven to 220°C. Place 1 generous tablespoon spinach mixture on top of each oyster in its shell and shape into a mound to cover oyster completely. Heat on top shelf of oven for 6–8 minutes, until top is slightly browned, spinach mixture is hot, and oysters are just warmed but not overcooked.

Salad of prawns, butter beans + watercress with prawn + tomato mayonnaise

Serves 6

18 large green prawns
¼ cup chopped basil leaves
¼ cup extra-virgin olive oil
1 clove garlic, finely chopped
2 tablespoons strained lemon juice
10 drops Tabasco sauce
pinch cayenne pepper
salt, to taste
500 g butter beans, topped and tailed
1 bunch watercress
juice of 1 lemon, extra, strained

Prawn & tomato mayonnaise

1 tablespoon extra-virgin olive oil
1 golden shallot, finely chopped
1 clove garlic, finely chopped
250 g tomatoes, blanched (see page 174),
    peeled, seeded and finely chopped
200 ml light olive oil*
200 g green prawn heads, reserved
    from above
2 egg yolks
1 tablespoon strained lemon juice
½ teaspoon salt
Tabasco sauce, to taste
cayenne pepper, to taste

✳ If you don't have light olive oil on hand,
use half extra-virgin olive oil and half
flavourless vegetable oil, as a mayonnaise
made using only extra-virgin olive oil
tends to have too strong a flavour.

The doyenne of the Australian food scene, Joan Campbell, wrote in *Bloody Delicious!*: 'If you know how to cook a . . . bean you know how to cook anything.' I'd love to know who started the craze of cooking beans for just a minute, so that they remain raw. Vegetables such as beans and asparagus must be boiled long enough to make the transformation from raw to cooked but remain al dente. It's true, there's a fine line between a raw bean and an overcooked one, but eating a bean that is still crunchy is, to me, like eating undercooked pasta.

Peel and devein prawns, leaving the tails intact and reserving 200 g of the heads for the prawn & tomato mayonnaise. Combine basil, olive oil, garlic, 2 tablespoons lemon juice, Tabasco sauce, cayenne pepper and salt. Add prawns and refrigerate for 30 minutes–1 hour.

Meanwhile, make the mayonnaise by heating the extra-virgin olive oil in a small frying pan. Add shallot and garlic, and fry until very lightly browned. Add tomatoes and cook over a high heat until reduced to ½ cup. Set aside to cool. Combine light olive oil and reserved prawn heads in a saucepan. Bring to the boil, reduce heat to medium and cook for 5 minutes, constantly crushing the heads with a wooden spoon or, ideally, a pestle. Set aside to cool. Pass through a fine sieve, pressing down firmly on the mixture to extract as much flavour as possible from the solids. Discard solids – you should end up with about 175 ml prawn oil. Whisk egg yolks, lemon juice and salt in a small bowl. While whisking, slowly add the prawn oil, drop by drop at first, then in a slow, steady stream, until all the oil is incorporated. Stir in tomato mixture. Taste and add extra salt, Tabasco and cayenne pepper to taste – I prefer it quite hot. Refrigerate until required.

Heat a flat barbecue plate or heavy-based frying pan until very hot. Remove prawns from marinade, place on barbecue or in frying pan, cook for 1 minute, then turn and cook for a further minute. Remove from heat and set aside to cool.

Bring a large saucepan of salted water to the boil, add butter beans and cook for 6–8 minutes, until tender. Drain, refresh in cold water and set aside to cool. Pick 2 handfuls of sprigs from the watercress, then toss with beans in the remaining lemon juice.

Place a handful of beans and watercress in a mound on each plate. Arrange 3 prawns on top and drizzle over a generous amount of mayonnaise.

Slow-poached veal liver with bitter greens + crisp pork fat

Serves 6

1.5 kg veal liver
2 teaspoons salt
1 tablespoon Quatre Épices (see page 178)
1 tablespoon chopped thyme leaves
1 clove garlic, chopped
½ cup finely chopped flat-leaf parsley leaves
1 cup extra-virgin olive oil
6 cups bitter greens (such as curly endive, radicchio, chicory, witlof and dandelion)
300 g salt pork fat*
6 tablespoons red wine vinegar
salt flakes, to taste
freshly ground black pepper, to taste

✱ Some butchers carry salt pork fat, as do Spanish and Portuguese delicatessens. If salt pork fat is unavailable, most butchers sell thin slices of pork back fat. Sprinkle liberally with salt and refrigerate overnight. Or make your own: cover a 1 kg piece pork back fat with salt and refrigerate for 1–2 weeks before use.

While some cooks today look for lean pork, pork fat has long been one of the most valuable ingredients in many cuisines. Where would sausages be without pork fat? Where would lean cuts of meat be without lardons of pork fat to keep them moist? And I can't think of rillettes in their pots without the appetising sealing layer of translucent pork fat. The liver must be cooked at an accurate temperature, so you will need a meat thermometer; under- or overcooked liver won't work.

Carefully remove outside membrane from the liver, then cut off and discard a thin slice (about 1 cm) from the flat side to remove as many of the veins as possible. Trim into a neat rectangular shape – you should end up with about 1 kg liver (you can use the off-cuts in another dish, such as a pasta sauce). Insert a meat thermometer into the centre of the liver then place in a freezer bag with the 2 teaspoons salt, Quatre Épices, thyme, garlic, parsley and olive oil, and seal bag tightly, squeezing out excess air. Place bag in a large saucepan with 4 litres water and heat until thermometer reads 60°C (don't open the bag – you should be able to read the thermometer through the plastic), then immediately remove saucepan from heat and leave liver, in bag, to cool in the water.

Wash and dry greens then divide among 6 plates. Remove liver from freezer bag and cut carefully into 12 slices. Place 2 slices on each plate on top of greens.

Dust excess salt off the salt pork fat and slice thinly. Heat a frying pan, then add slices of pork fat and toss until they melt a little and start to become crisp. Remove crisp fat, drain on kitchen paper and keep warm. Add red wine vinegar to the same pan and boil for 1 minute. Drizzle pork fat and boiled red wine vinegar mixture over greens and liver – you may not need to use all of it – then top with pieces of crisped pork fat, a sprinkling of salt flakes (depending on how salty the salt pork is) and a grinding of black pepper.

Salt-cured duck with fresh + lightly pickled melons

Serves 6
1 kg salt
3 litres water
12 cloves, crushed
6 star anise, crushed
1.5 cm knob ginger, chopped
2 × 1.5–2 kg Peking ducks, necks and
    wings removed
1 teaspoon Quatre Épices (see page 178)
4 × 25 cm squares muslin
kitchen twine
¼ honeydew melon
¼ rockmelon

Lightly pickled melons
¼ honeydew melon
¼ rockmelon
150 ml water
150 ml white wine vinegar
80 g white sugar
½ teaspoon cloves, crushed
½ teaspoon coriander seeds, crushed
1 tablespoon chopped ginger
½ bird's-eye chilli, chopped

The development of this recipe was a journey that started when I read about salt-water duck in Elizabeth David's *Spices, Salt and Aromatics in the English Kitchen*. Here she poaches duck whole for 1 hour and, when cold, chops it into pieces with a cleaver and serves it with a salad. After years of twists and turns I adapted her recipe into this dish. The Peking duck used here is a breed of duck, not the Chinese dish of duck cooked with a lacquered skin and wrapped in thin pancakes with strips of cucumber and spring onion. The English Aylesbury duck, which is a very similar breed, could also be used here. You'll need to start this dish the day before you want to serve it, to salt the duck and pickle the melons.

The day before, make pickled melons by peeling melons and slicing thinly. Arrange slices, overlapping, on a non-aluminium baking dish. Combine the water, vinegar, sugar, cloves, coriander seeds, ginger and chilli in a small saucepan and boil for 2 minutes. Strain the hot marinade over the fruit. Cover and refrigerate for 24 hours.

To start curing the ducks, dissolve salt in water in a non-aluminium container. Add cloves, star anise, ginger and ducks. Place a plate on the water surface to keep the ducks submerged, and refrigerate for 24 hours.

The next day, drain, dry, halve and bone the ducks, removing as much fat as possible without damaging the skin or flesh. Sprinkle the flesh with Quatre Épices. Roll each duck half into a fat sausage shape, about 12 × 5 cm. Wrap each roll in a muslin square and secure well with plenty of kitchen twine. Bring a large saucepan of water to the boil, reduce heat to a gentle simmer, add the duck rolls and poach for 15 minutes. Insert a thin metal skewer into the centre of one of the rolls and place the tip on your lower lip – it should be just hot. If not, cook for a further 5 minutes and test again. When rolls are cooked, drain and allow to cool, then refrigerate until very cold.

Meanwhile, peel the fresh melons and slice thinly. When the duck rolls are cold, remove from muslin and slice as thinly as possible. Place slices of roll on plates with alternate layers of fresh and lightly pickled melons alongside. Strain the melon pickling juices and spoon a little over the duck and fruit.

Salad of prosciutto, figs, melon + macerated mint cream

Serves 6
30 mint leaves
3 tablespoons strained lemon juice
½ cup 35%-fat cream
½ cup 45%-fat cream
½ teaspoon salt
12 large or 18 small figs, peeled
1 cup diced rockmelon
15 slices prosciutto

I look forward to fig season each year, and to the superb dish of figs wrapped in prosciutto and baked with gorgonzola that my friend Armando Percuoco serves at Ristorante Buon Ricordo in Paddington, Sydney. Use figs only well into the season, when they're ripe and sweet (and less expensive), and peel them for this recipe. I don't remember eating unpeeled figs in Greece when I was a child, but I do recall fig seasons when all the children would progress from one neighbour's tree to another's, until we were finally sick from eating so many figs. This salad appeared on the MG Garage menu whenever figs were in season.

Macerate (soak) 24 of the mint leaves in the lemon juice for 10 minutes. Cut remaining mint leaves into thin strips and set aside. Drain the soaked mint leaves, squeezing as much lemon juice from them as possible, then discard the leaves and retain the lemon juice. Combine the creams, add retained lemon juice and the salt, and whip until soft peaks form. Slice a cross in the top of each fig and fill with 1 teaspoon diced rockmelon. Cut 3 slices of the prosciutto into thin strips.

Place 2–3 figs on each plate and wrap them loosely in 2 whole slices of prosciutto. Pour 1 dessertspoon macerated mint cream over each fig, and sprinkle over strips of prosciutto and mint.

Quail + pig's trotter sausage in vine leaves with iceberg lettuce

Serves 6

3 pig's trotters*
6 cloves garlic, roughly chopped
3 cm piece ginger, sliced
1 medium carrot, roughly chopped
1 small brown onion, roughly chopped
½ stick celery, roughly chopped
2 sprigs thyme
1 dried bay leaf
salt, to taste
Ras El Hanout (see page 177), to taste
6 × 200 g quail
12 pickled vine leaves
6 × 25 cm squares muslin
kitchen twine
2 teaspoons grated ginger
¼ cup chopped spring onions,
    green part only
2 teaspoons honey
olive oil, for deep-frying
3 pickled vine leaves, extra
1 small iceberg lettuce, cut into 6 wedges
1 lemon
extra-virgin olive oil, for serving

✱ If pig's trotters are not to your taste, stuff the quail with chicken livers and use chicken stock instead of the trotter stock, although you won't get the same gelatinous effect. I've also used calf's feet instead of the trotters (see page 104 for guidance on dealing with veal hoof).

There are very few dishes that can be called totally new; most dishes have been inspired by an earlier dish in some way. And this sausage has evolved over many years, from my days at Berowra Waters Inn and then at Bennelong, to this incarnation with the Greek touch of vine leaves, which became a signature dish at MG Garage. This recipe assumes you will use whole quail, but you can ask your poultry supplier to bone them for you.

If the trotters still have any hairs on them, hold them over an open flame to singe off hairs, taking care not to singe the meat, as this will impart a horrible taste. To blanch trotters and remove any impurities, wash them well under running water, place in a large saucepan, cover with water, and bring to the boil. Discard water and rinse trotters again. Combine trotters, garlic, sliced ginger, carrot, onion, celery, thyme and bay leaf in a large saucepan, cover with water and bring to the boil. Reduce heat, then cover and simmer for 2–3 hours, until meat falls off the bone. Remove trotters from stock and wrap immediately in plastic film. Strain and reserve the stock. As soon as the trotters are cool enough to handle, unwrap them, then remove and retain all meat, taking care to remove the very small bones.

Season meat liberally with salt and Ras El Hanout, then pack into a rectangular dish to a depth of 2 cm. Refrigerate until set, then cut into 6 large finger-sized batons ready for stuffing the quail.

Bone quail and season with Ras El Hanout and salt. Place a baton of the trotter meat in the middle of each boned quail and wrap in 2 vine leaves to form a fat sausage shape. Wrap each sausage firmly in a piece of muslin and tie with plenty of kitchen twine, so that the sausage keeps its shape during cooking. Bring a large saucepan of water to the boil, plunge sausages into it and cook for 3 minutes. Transfer cooked sausages to a small pan just large enough to hold them all, then add grated ginger, spring onions, honey and 100 ml of the reserved trotter stock. Bring to the boil, cover, reduce heat and simmer for 5 minutes. Remove from heat, allow to cool, then refrigerate in pan.

Preheat oven to 220°C. Remove sausages from muslin, place on a non-stick baking tray and bake for about 5 minutes, until warmed through. Heat oil and deep-fry the sausages to crisp them on the outside. Drain sausages on kitchen paper and fry the extra vine leaves for a minute, removing them as soon as they stop sizzling (if you leave them any longer they will become bitter) and draining them on kitchen paper. Cut each hot sausage diagonally into 3 pieces. Serve with iceberg lettuce wedges, a squeeze of lemon juice and a drizzle of olive oil, with fried vine leaves crumbled over the top.

Salad of brisket, pig's ear cartilage + green elk

Serves 6

1 kg corned brisket
1 large brown onion, roughly chopped
½ stick celery, roughly chopped
1 large carrot, roughly chopped
2 sprigs thyme
2 dried bay leaves
½ cup white wine vinegar
½ teaspoon black peppercorns
10 coriander seeds
10 cloves
1 stick cinnamon
½ teaspoon yellow mustard seeds
3 tablespoons small salted capers,
    blanched (see page 174)
6 cornichons (see page 172), sliced
1 small telegraph cucumber, peeled and
    cut into thin strips
6 golden shallots, finely sliced
salt, to taste
freshly ground black pepper, to taste
6 cups green elk*
Dijon Mustard Vinaigrette (see page 178),
    to taste

Pig's ears

3 pig's ears
1 small brown onion, roughly chopped
½ small stick celery, roughly chopped
50 g ginger, roughly chopped
6 cloves garlic, peeled
5 star anise
1 tablespoon chopped flat-leaf parsley
    leaves
salt, to taste
freshly ground black pepper, to taste

✱ If you can't find green elk, peppery greens are best, but try any salad green, such as winter purslane, rocket, mizuna or watercress.

Pigs have been described as the animal you eat from nose to tail, and in my cooking career I certainly have used every part of this animal. Dare I say that at the Bennelong I served a salad made from different parts of the pig, including the testicles? That was the first time I'd cooked with pig's ear cartilage. It was understandably a difficult dish to describe on the menu, and finally appeared as 'Salad of Pig's Bits'. The pig's ear cartilage in this salad adds a wonderful texture, as it so often does in Chinese dishes.

Cover brisket with water in a large saucepan and bring to the boil, to blanch and remove impurities. Drain and refresh with cold water. Put into a clean saucepan with onion, celery, carrot, thyme, bay leaves, vinegar, peppercorns, coriander seeds, cloves, cinnamon, mustard seeds and enough water to cover. Bring to the boil, reduce heat and simmer, covered, for 2–3 hours, until tender. Allow brisket to cool in the cooking liquid then refrigerate in pan until cold.

Meanwhile, singe any hairs off the pig's ears by holding them over an open flame with a pair of tongs. Don't leave them over the flame any longer than necessary, as if the skin burns it will have an unpleasant taste. Wash thoroughly and place in a saucepan with onion, celery, ginger, garlic, star anise and enough water to cover. Bring to the boil, reduce heat and simmer, covered, for 2–3 hours, until a skewer goes through the ear cartilage. Leave ears in the cooking liquid until cool enough to handle, then scrape off skin and keep it warm. Cut cartilage in half, stack all the pieces on top of each other, wrap tightly in plastic film and refrigerate with a weight on top.

Mix parsley, salt and pepper through the warm skin from the ears. Form into a sausage shape on a piece of plastic film and wrap up tightly. Refrigerate until cold.

Drain brisket well, discard fatty part and shred the lean meat into long strips with your fingers – you should end up with about 3 cups shredded meat. Place meat in a large bowl.

Cut compressed pig's ear cartilage into paper-thin shavings with a sharp knife and add to bowl. Unwrap the pig's ear skin, slice into thin discs and add to bowl. Add capers, cornichons, cucumber, shallots, salt and pepper. Add enough vinaigrette to moisten then toss gently with your fingers. Taste and add extra salt and pepper if required.

In a separate bowl, toss green elk with a small amount of vinaigrette. Place a ring of green elk on each plate with a mound of the meat salad in the centre.

Main

Courses

Elizabeth David

A. ESCOFFIER A GUIDE TO MODERN COOKERY

ΜΑΓΕΙΡΙΚΗ

If I had just one cookbook it would be *The Margaret Fulton Cookbook*. And if I was allowed only one more, it would be Stephanie Alexander's *Cook's Companion*. A third would have to be *Escoffier: The Complete Guide to the Art of Modern Cookery*. If I were to extend my library to 10 cookbooks, Elizabeth David's and Jane Grigson's would definitely be among them. But I have 500 cookbooks, and despite my reading difficulties I've skimmed through all of them. Being a self-taught cook, cookbooks have played an important part in my career. Where would I be if I hadn't read pages and pages of detailed instructions on how to make the perfect omelette or soufflé in *Mastering the Art of French Cooking* by Julia Child, Louisette Bertholle and Simone Beck? In recent years I've become interested in Paula Wolfert's cookbooks. In the restaurant, I always had *Escoffier* (the culinary genius of our time) handy, a very well-worn copy of Stephanie's *Cook's Companion* (as in just about every kitchen I know of, professional or amateur), *Larousse Gastronomique* (as a quick reference), and the most instructive cookbooks from the Time Life series *The Good Cook: Techniques and Recipes*, 27 of them in all (now, sadly, out of print).

Talking of books, one day I had an idea for a dish and vaguely remembered cooking something similar 30 years ago from a Robert Carrier recipe. So I took two of his paperback cookbooks to work that evening to check the details. What a coincidence – the old man was visiting Australia briefly and was dining in the restaurant that night. Of course I took the books out to him and asked him to sign them, which he was very pleased to do. He went on to tell me how happy he was with his meal and ask how I'd managed to cook the individual coulibiac (which he'd had as his main course) without leaving a gap between the pancake-wrapped salmon and the brioche. That's right, I thought, when one cooks meat or fish in pastry there is normally a little gap between the pastry and the filling. So what was I doing wrong that was so right? I went back into the kitchen thinking about it and later cooked two extra coulibiac to see exactly what happens. I discovered that because I always try to cook the salmon as rare as possible to keep it moist, it doesn't have time to shrink away from the pastry and create the usual gap. So next time you see a terrine in pastry with more jelly than it should have, you know the meat part is overcooked. Oh what a wonderful career I chose – one never stops learning!

Baked eggplant, pine nut + gruyère moussaka

Serves 8

2 kg eggplants
12 large Roma tomatoes, blanched
    (see page 174), peeled, halved
    and seeded
salt, to taste
freshly ground black pepper, to taste
olive oil, for frying
60 g butter
2 large brown onions, chopped
120 g parmesan cheese (see page 172),
    grated
160 g gruyère cheese, grated
1 teaspoon ground cinnamon
⅔ cup chopped flat-leaf parsley leaves
⅔ cup pine nuts, toasted (see page 174)
    and roughly chopped

Béchamel sauce

40 g butter
⅓ cup plain flour
1 litre milk
1½ teaspoons salt
1½ teaspoons freshly ground white pepper
¾ teaspoon freshly grated nutmeg
4 eggs, lightly beaten

✱ The moussaka can be prepared several
hours in advance, or even the day before,
up to the step of adding the béchamel
sauce. Keep refrigerated, but bring to
room temperature before cooking.

A traditional moussaka can often swim in olive oil, but this version is lighter. It's a complete meal, requiring only a small side salad. I often serve it with a Greek salad of olives, crumbled fetta, chopped tomato, chopped peeled cucumber, chopped green capsicum, parsley leaves, dried Greek oregano and a dressing of white wine vinegar, olive oil, salt and pepper. A true Greek salad never includes lettuce.

To make béchamel sauce, melt butter in a small saucepan, add flour and cook for 1–2 minutes over a medium heat, until mixture turns a sandy colour but not brown. Add milk slowly, stirring constantly, until sauce boils and thickens. Reduce heat and simmer gently for 10 minutes. Add salt, pepper and nutmeg. Remove from heat and, when cool, stir in eggs. Strain and refrigerate until required.

Preheat oven to 200°C. Place half the eggplants on a baking tray. Line another baking tray with baking paper, place tomatoes on it cut-side down, and sprinkle with olive oil, salt and pepper. Bake eggplants and tomatoes for about 30 minutes, until a skewer goes through eggplants easily. Remove cooked eggplants from oven, and continue cooking tomatoes for another 10 minutes or until they start to brown, then remove from oven and increase oven temperature to 220°C.

Meanwhile, slice remaining eggplants thinly, sprinkle with salt, leave for 30 minutes, then pat dry. Pour olive oil into a frying pan to a depth of 5 mm, heat oil, then fry eggplant slices in batches, in a single layer, until golden brown. Heat more oil and continue frying eggplant slices in batches until all are cooked. Drain on kitchen paper, patting well to remove excess oil.

Melt butter in a saucepan and cook onions until golden. Once the roasted eggplants are cool enough to handle, peel them and chop the flesh. Arrange half the eggplant slices in the bottom of a baking dish, or 8 individual dishes. Combine parmesan with half the gruyère and sprinkle half of this mixture over the eggplant slices. Arrange tomato halves over the cheese. Combine onions with chopped roasted eggplant, cinnamon, salt and pepper and spread over the tomatoes. Sprinkle over parsley, pine nuts and the remaining parmesan and gruyère mixture. Top with remaining eggplant slices then with béchamel sauce.✱ Sprinkle over remaining gruyère and bake for about 30 minutes for a large tray, or 20 minutes for individual dishes, until golden.

Serves 6

1 kg mixed bitter greens (such as nettles,*
    sorrel, silver beet, chicory)
150 ml extra-virgin olive oil
2 medium red onions, finely chopped
1 egg, lightly beaten
dried Greek oregano (see page 172),
    to taste
500 g fresh ricotta
salt, to taste
freshly ground black pepper, to taste
1 cup olive oil, extra, for brushing
plain flour, extra, for dusting

Filo pastry

500 g plain flour
225 ml warm water
1 egg, lightly beaten
1 teaspoon salt

✱ When preparing nettles, wear rubber
gloves, as any contact with your skin
will cause itchiness. Harvested from the
wild, only the young shoots and tops
of nettles are eaten, but they must be
cooked beforehand to remove the stinging
element. A long rolling pin the thickness
of a broomstick will open up the filo much
better than an ordinary rolling pin.

This type of pie is traditional in the north of Greece, where I grew up.
It uses a gathered pastry topping rather than a flat top, giving more of
that crisp pastry surface that's everyone's favourite part of a pie, isn't it?
I vividly remember watching my grandmother and her sister making this
pie when I was a child. At the time I couldn't understand the reason for the
circle of pastry that topped all the other irregular pieces while they were
rolling it out – why not just cut the dough into 9 squares, I thought, rather
than mess around with the plate and cutting out the circle first? When I
finally came to make the pie myself, many, many years later, I realised that
putting the oiled layers underneath the larger round piece meant the rolling
pin could move more easily, without slipping in the oil. Gathering wild
greens is a popular pastime in the villages of Greece; families will plan a
day's outing, with a picnic lunch, and scour the hillsides for edible greens,
mostly wild dandelions. The most tender greens are found in the shade of
the tall old cypress trees.

To make the filo pastry, combine all ingredients in a bowl and stir until they come
together in a dough. Transfer to a lightly floured surface and knead for 2–3 minutes or
until smooth. Wrap in plastic film and refrigerate for 1 hour.

    Wash greens and, with the water still clinging to them, place in a saucepan, then
cover and cook over medium heat until just wilted. Drain in a colander and squeeze to
extract as much liquid as possible. Chop roughly and set aside in a bowl.➔

Heat 150 ml olive oil in the same saucepan and cook onions over a low heat for 8–10 minutes, until soft. Remove from heat and combine with greens, then add egg and oregano. Gently fold in ricotta, season with salt and pepper, cover and refrigerate.

Preheat oven to 200°C. Cut filo pastry dough in half and roll out* one half on a lightly floured surface into a 60 cm square (you can also use your hands to stretch the pastry as you are rolling, to make it easier). Using a dinner plate as a guide, cut a round from the centre of the pastry, then cut remaining pastry into 8 equal pieces and brush these 8 pieces liberally with the extra olive oil.

Place the 8 pastry pieces on top of one another (see photo 1), top with the pastry round, dust generously with flour and roll out into a 40 cm round, trimming edges to neaten. (Don't worry about oil spilling out from the sides of the pastry as you roll. There will be mess, but you can clean up later!) Place this round on a 26 cm pizza tray lined with baking paper. Repeat rolling, cutting and layering with the remaining pastry half, trimming edges to make a neat 40 cm round. Set aside.

Spread filling to edges of pizza tray, then fold excess pastry over filling, pleating sides as you go (see photo 2). Gently gather second sheet of rolled pastry with both hands and place on top of pie, allowing it to fall into folds (see photo 3). Brush generously with olive oil and bake for 30 minutes or until golden. Serve warm or at room temperature.

Baked barramundi with tomato, potato + a sea urchin sauce

Serves 6

1 kg medium potatoes*
250 g butter, melted
salt, to taste
freshly ground white pepper, to taste
3 tablespoons finely chopped flat-leaf
    parsley leaves
12 Roma tomatoes, blanched (see page
    174), peeled, quartered and seeded
6 × 150 g steaks wild barramundi, skin on

Sea urchin sauce

1 cup dry white wine
2½ tablespoons white wine vinegar
1 tablespoon 35%-fat cream
250 g cold salted butter, cubed
30 tongues sea urchin roe

* You don't want potatoes that are either
too waxy or too floury for this dish.
Something in between, like a desiree,
is perfect.

The sea urchins in the Mediterranean are small, and fishermen and restaurants snip the tops off them with a specially made pair of scissors resembling a very large cigar-cutter. Australian sea urchins, however, are much larger, with a thicker shell. I used to split them in half with a cleaver, but this method was a bit rough and didn't always leave all the tongues of roe intact (each sea urchin contains 5 tongues of roe). So I came up with an idea straight from my electrician's toolbox. After cutting the sea urchin's mouth away with a small knife, I placed a pair of pliers into the hole and used them to prise the shell apart. It fell naturally into 2 pieces, one containing 3 perfect tongues of roe and the other containing 2.

Place potatoes in a saucepan, cover with cold water and boil for about 15 minutes, until a skewer goes through them easily – do not overcook or they will be difficult to slice. Drain, cool and peel. Slice thinly.

Meanwhile, start sauce. Combine wine and vinegar in a small saucepan, bring to the boil, reduce to 1 tablespoon and set saucepan aside.

Preheat oven to 220°C. Line a 30 × 20 cm baking tray with baking paper and brush paper with a little of the melted butter. Lay potato slices on the tray, overlapping slightly. Brush generously with melted butter, then sprinkle with salt, pepper and parsley. Arrange tomato quarters, cut-side down, on top of the potatoes. Brush gently with melted butter and set aside.

Line another 30 × 20 cm baking tray with baking paper and brush with a little melted butter. Place barramundi on tray, brush with melted butter and sprinkle with salt and pepper. Place potato tray in the oven for 10 minutes. Add barramundi tray and cook both for another 10 minutes, until tomatoes have browned slightly.

Meanwhile finish the sauce. Mix cream into reduced wine and vinegar and place over a medium heat. Whisk butter, piece by piece, into the sauce, ensuring that the sauce doesn't get too hot, or it will split. Remove from heat and add tongues of sea urchin roe, stirring gently to combine without breaking them.

Cut potato and tomato bake into 6 portions and place a portion on each plate. Top with a piece of fish and spoon over sauce, ensuring that each serve receives 5 tongues of sea urchin roe.

Semolina-crusted flounder with white asparagus + ravigote sauce

Serves 6

6 × 350 g flounder,* scaled, gilled
    and gutted
1 tablespoon extra-virgin olive oil
6 red radishes, thinly sliced
1 teaspoon white wine vinegar
18 spears white asparagus
2 tablespoons butter, melted
½ cup fine semolina
salt, to taste
freshly ground black pepper, to taste
Clarified Butter (see page 175), for frying
12–18 boiled small potatoes, to serve

Ravigote sauce

2 teaspoons seeded mustard
2 tablespoons white wine vinegar
2 tablespoons small salted capers,
    blanched (see page 174)
2 tablespoons chopped flat-leaf parsley
    leaves
2 tablespoons sliced cornichons
    (see page 172)
1 tablespoon chopped French tarragon
    leaves
1 tablespoon finely chopped golden
    shallots
100 ml extra-virgin olive oil
salt, to taste
freshly ground black pepper, to taste

✱ Any flat fish, such as John dory or sole,
will work well in this recipe.

I love flounder. It's found in waters all around Australia and I wonder why people don't cook it more often. Perhaps because it's almost always sold whole, rarely as fillets, and people are a bit daunted by that. This is a delicious recipe from the MG Garage menu, but some people might find the preparation of the flounder a bit fiddly. One flounder dish we often enjoy at home is as simple as laying the whole fish on a baking tray lined with baking paper, adding a tablespoon of Noilly Prat vermouth, a knob of butter, 2–3 slices of lemon or lime, a sprig of dill, salt and pepper. Cover the tray with foil and bake at 200°C for about 20 minutes, until cooked. Serve flounder with its juices and some mashed or steamed potatoes – it makes a great quick dinner.

Cut the heads off the flounder. With a small, thin knife, make an incision between the flesh and the belly fin on both sides of the fin. Gently pull on the fin, removing it and the small bones that are attached to it. Repeat with the top (dorsal) fin. You should be left with both sides of the fish joined by the backbone and tail, with all the other bones removed. Trim the end of the tail.

Make the ravigote sauce by combining all ingredients and mixing well. Set aside.

Meanwhile, heat the olive oil in a small frying pan and cook radishes over a medium heat until just soft. Remove from heat, add vinegar (so they retain their colour) and set aside.

Cut the woody ends off the asparagus spears and peel the remaining bottom halves. Cook in boiling salted water for about 8 minutes, depending on size, until tender. Drain, brush with melted butter and keep warm.

Coat flounder in semolina, salt and pepper. Heat Clarified Butter in 2 large frying pans and fry 3 flounder in each pan for 2–3 minutes each side, until golden. (If it seems too tricky to cook in 2 frying pans at once, cook 3 flounder and keep them warm in a low oven while you cook the other 3.)

Stir radishes through ravigote sauce. Serve flounder with asparagus and boiled small potatoes, and pass the ravigote sauce separately.

Grilled tommy ruff with fresh tomato, olive + herb sauce

Serves 6
18 × 60 g tommy ruff fillets,* skin on
extra-virgin olive oil, for brushing
salt, to taste
freshly ground white pepper, to taste

Fresh tomato, olive & herb sauce
150 ml extra-virgin olive oil
2½ tablespoons white wine vinegar
6 small tomatoes, blanched (see page 174),
    peeled, seeded and chopped
1 cup Ligurian olives,* pitted and chopped
1 teaspoon coriander seeds, ground
1 teaspoon fennel seeds, ground
salt, to taste
freshly ground white pepper, to taste
2 tablespoons snipped chives
2 tablespoons chopped flat-leaf parsley
    leaves
2 tablespoons torn basil leaves
2 tablespoons chopped thyme leaves

❋ Tommy ruff, also known as Australian
herring, is less common on the east coast;
you can easily substitute red mullet or
large sardines. You can use any small black
olives in this dish. To remove olive flesh
from the stones, place them between 2 tea
towels and hit them gently with the palm
of your hand or a meat mallet.

While I was running the kitchen at Bennelong I met Ben Fitton, a 17-year-old apprentice. He had just arrived from Coffs Harbour to do his apprenticeship in the big city, and was full of enthusiasm and eager to learn everything about cooking. He later became my chef at Fuel Bistro, and I had so much faith in him that some of the specials on the menu were his creations. The recipe below is one of them.

To make the sauce, pour oil and vinegar into a small saucepan. Bring to the boil, then add tomato, olives, ground coriander, ground fennel, salt and pepper, and return to the boil. Remove from heat and stir through herbs. Set aside.

Place fillets, skin-side up, on a baking tray lined with baking paper. Brush liberally with olive oil and sprinkle with salt and pepper. Place under a hot grill for a couple of minutes until skin starts to blister.

Place 3 fillets on each plate and pour over a little sauce.

Serves 6

1 large bulb fennel
1 cup Fish Stock* (see page 175)
12 baby carrots, halved
12 salad onions,* halved
3 × 700 g whole snapper, scaled, gutted
    and filleted, carcasses reserved for
    Fish Stock*
12 sugar snap peas

Avgolemono sauce

6 egg yolks
2 cloves garlic
3 tablespoons strained lemon juice
salt, to taste
freshly ground white pepper, to taste
½ cup light olive oil*
600 ml hot Fish Stock (see page 175)

✻ Salad onions are immature onions with
a partially developed bulb. If you make the
Fish Stock freshly for this dish, you can
use the carcasses left over from filleting
the snapper. You can also combine some of
the oil skimmed from the stock with light
olive oil to make up the ½ cup oil required
for the avgolemono.

Avgo means 'egg' and *lemono* means 'lemons'. Avgolemono is a traditional Greek sauce made by whisking egg and lemon juice together, and is usually poured into hot soups to thicken them. It's used so often by Greeks that it sometimes seems to be the only sauce in Greek cooking. One of my favourite dishes is youvarlakia, meatballs made from rice and minced veal cooked in a light stock that is then thickened with avgolemono: a hearty meatball soup. My avgolemono here is a cross between a traditional Greek avgolemono and a French bourride – a white seafood soup flavoured with garlic mayonnaise (aïoli).

To make the avgolemono sauce, combine egg yolks, garlic, lemon juice, salt and pepper in a blender or food processor. With the motor still running, gradually add the oil, drop by drop at first, then in a slow, steady stream, until all oil is incorporated. Keep the motor running, and carefully and slowly add hot Fish Stock until all is incorporated.

Cut tender green sprigs from fennel tops and reserve for garnish. Slice fennel bulb into 12 wedges. Pour the Fish Stock into a large, deep frying pan, add carrots, salad onions and fennel, then bring to the boil. Reduce heat, cover and simmer for a few minutes, until carrots and onions are almost tender, then lay fish fillets and sugar snap peas on top. Continue to simmer, covered, for a few more minutes, carefully turning fish once, until fish is just cooked.

Remove fish and vegetables from the frying pan, leaving the liquid, and divide among 6 heated soup bowls. Add the avgolemono sauce to the stock in the frying pan and whisk, over high heat, until hot and frothy. Pour sauce over the snapper and vegetables and garnish with a few fennel sprigs.

Baked whiting with leeks, orange + herbs

Serves 6

1 cup extra-virgin olive oil
3 leeks, white part only, washed well
    and sliced
1 large carrot, cut into thin strips
2 sticks celery, sliced
3 cloves garlic, chopped
1 teaspoon coriander seeds, ground
1 teaspoon fennel seeds, ground
salt, to taste
freshly ground white pepper, to taste
12 × 100 g whiting fillets,* skin on,
    bones removed
2 tablespoons roughly chopped flat-leaf
    parsley leaves
1 tablespoon roughly chopped basil leaves
1 tablespoon snipped chives
2 teaspoons roughly chopped French
    tarragon leaves
1 orange, cut into 12 thin slices
½ cup strained orange juice

* I have also cooked this dish using red mullet, snapper and garfish. The vegetable mixture can be used to stuff a large fish, such as whole snapper.

A few years back, when Gordon Ramsay was a guest chef at Brisbane Masterclass, I didn't have much interest in seeing his session. Journalist Cherry Ripe was writing an article on him, however, and encouraged me to go along with her. Curiosity got the better of me and I found myself sitting in the front row. Between Ramsay insulting the audience and throwing flour over Cherry's photographer's camera, the session was actually quite informative, and I learnt one little trick that I have used ever since. Before lining anything with baking paper, Ramsay wet the paper to make it more pliable. Very simple but very effective – and it just goes to show, we can always learn something new.

Preheat oven to 200°C. Heat half the olive oil in a saucepan and fry the leeks until golden. Add the carrot, celery and garlic and cook until just soft. Add half the ground coriander seeds, half the ground fennel seeds, salt and pepper, and allow to cool. Place vegetable mixture on a large baking tray or in 6 small gratin dishes, and place the fish on top, skin-side up. Sprinkle fish with more salt, pepper and the remaining ground coriander and fennel seeds. Combine herbs and sprinkle over the fish. Halve the orange slices and place 2 halves on top of each fillet. Pour orange juice and remaining olive oil over the fish. Wet a piece of baking paper and screw it up, to make it more pliable. Flatten it out and use it to cover the fish. Bake for about 15 minutes, until fish is cooked through.

Sicilian stuffed red mullet with grilled lemons + parsley salad

Serves 6
1 lemon, thinly sliced
salt, to taste
extra-virgin olive oil, for preserving lemons
6 × 250 g red mullet, butterflied*
    (see page 174)
1 cup plain flour
2 eggs, lightly beaten
1¼ cups Gremolata Breadcrumbs
    (see page 175)
Clarified Butter (see page 175), for
    shallow-frying

Sicilian stuffing
2 tablespoons toasted (see page 174)
    and finely chopped pine nuts
3 tablespoons currants
juice of ½ lemon, strained
¼ cup Gremolata Breadcrumbs
    (see page 175)
salt, to taste
freshly ground black pepper, to taste

Parsley salad
2 cloves garlic, finely chopped
grated zest of 1 lemon
200 g Ligurian olives, pitted*
100 g golden shallots, chopped
50 g drained anchovy fillets (see page 172),
    chopped
2 firmly packed cups flat-leaf parsley
    leaves, very roughly chopped
½ cup extra-virgin olive oil
⅓ cup small salted capers, blanched
    (see page 174)
2 tablespoons strained lemon juice
1 teaspoon freshly ground black pepper

✱ You can ask your fishmonger to
butterfly the fish for you. Two large
sardine fillets per person also work well.
To remove olive flesh from the stones,
place them between 2 tea towels and hit
them gently with the palm of your hand or
a meat mallet.

Some of the best dishes have been created by accident or in an emergency. The parsley salad served here is one such dish. One night during a very busy service we ran out of appetisers, so I quickly threw together a few ingredients to make a small salad that could be served on a slice of melba toast. It was such a hit that it appeared afterwards on the menu in many variations. It can also be served in small tart cases as a canapé. You'll need to start the lemons the day before for this dish, although you could use my Preserved Lemons (see page 178), as we did at MG Garage.

The day before, carefully remove all seeds from lemon slices. Sprinkle with salt and leave for 1 hour. Pat dry and store in olive oil overnight.

Combine all stuffing ingredients and mix thoroughly. Trim tail fins from mullet and remove any pin bones, then stuff each fish with a sixth of the stuffing. Coat fish in flour, then egg, then Gremolata Breadcrumbs. Heat Clarified Butter in a frying pan and at the same time heat a barbecue grill or cast-iron pan until very hot. Fry fish in frying pan for a few minutes each side, until breadcrumbs are golden. Meanwhile, remove 6 lemon slices from the oil and cook on the grill or cast-iron pan until well browned.

Combine all salad ingredients. Share salad among the plates, top with a red mullet and add a grilled lemon slice on top.

Pepper-crusted Spanish mackerel with celeriac + salmon roe mayonnaise

Serves 6

6 × 200 g steaks Spanish mackerel,* skin on
olive oil, for pan-frying
2 large celeriac,* cut into thin strips

Black pepper coating

2 tablespoons cracked black peppercorns
1 tablespoon coriander seeds, finely ground
1 tablespoon fennel seeds, finely ground

Salmon roe mayonnaise

100 g salmon roe
1 clove garlic, chopped
2 tablespoons strained lemon juice
2 tablespoons water
1 teaspoon freshly ground white pepper
salt, to taste, depending on saltiness of roe
200 ml light olive oil

✽ If Spanish mackerel is not available, any firm-fleshed fish may be used, such as mahi mahi, swordfish or blue eye. In summer, when celeriac isn't available, substitute 2 telegraph cucumbers (peeled, seeded and cut into ribbons), 1 medium daikon (cut into ribbons) and 1 stick celery (finely sliced).

The first time I put this dish on the menu, I called it 'Pepper Steak of Mackerel', a play on the classic pepper steak. It created some debate as to whether a piece of fish can be called a 'steak'. According to my fishmonger, a 'fillet' is the whole side of a fish cut off the bone, a 'cutlet' is a piece of fish cut through the backbone so that it contains the bone, and a 'steak' is a piece cut from a fillet, usually from a large fish such as kingfish, swordfish, marlin or mackerel.

To make the mayonnaise, thoroughly combine half the salmon roe with the remaining mayonnaise ingredients, except the olive oil, in a blender. With motor still running, add olive oil slowly, drop by drop at first, then in a slow, steady stream, until all oil is incorporated. Remove from blender and fold through remaining salmon roe.

Preheat oven to 200°C. Trim any blood-lines (the dark parts) from the fish. Combine the black pepper coating ingredients on a small, flat plate. Coat the flesh side of the fish (side opposite the skin side) by rubbing it into the pepper mixture to form a thick crust. Heat an ovenproof frying pan and add olive oil to a depth of about 2 mm. When oil is very hot, sear the pepper coating, then turn fish to sear both ends, and then turn skin-side down. Place frying pan in oven, with the fish standing on its skin side, for about 15 minutes, until fish is cooked through.

Meanwhile, put 2 tablespoons water in a saucepan and add celeriac, then cover and steam over a high heat for 1 minute. Drain and toss through enough of the salmon roe mayonnaise to coat. Divide celeriac among 6 plates, top with fish and add an extra dollop of mayonnaise. You could also pass the mayonnaise separately.

Skate with pancetta, ginger sauce + fried cartilage

Serves 6

6 × 200 g skate wings
salt, to taste
freshly ground black pepper, to taste
12 thin slices flat pancetta
100 g caul fat (see page 172)
vegetable oil, for shallow-frying

Stuffing

600 g large field mushrooms
125 g butter
4 golden shallots, finely chopped
½ teaspoon finely chopped ginger
salt, to taste
freshly ground black pepper, to taste
2 teaspoons chopped coriander leaves

Ginger sauce

2 tablespoons butter
1 small brown onion, chopped
1 clove garlic, chopped
2 cm cube ginger, sliced
2 tablespoons plain flour
2 cups Fish or Chicken Stock
    (see pages 175–6)
salt, to taste
freshly ground white pepper, to taste

For this recipe I prefer the rounded brown skate wings, but you can also use the dark-skinned, V-shaped wings from very small rays, which are thicker. Skate is a very forgiving fish to cook – that is, it's hard to overcook. At MG Garage I made this dish with orange pine mushrooms, but they're only available for a short period, so I've substituted field mushrooms here; if you can get some pine mushrooms, all the better.

To make the stuffing, wipe the mushrooms with a damp cloth, peel the caps and remove the stalks, reserving peel and stalks. Slice caps and set aside. Chop stems and peelings. Melt a third of the butter in a frying pan, add a quarter of the shallots and cook until soft. Add the mushroom stems and peelings and cook over a medium heat until dry. Add ginger, salt, pepper and half the coriander, then set aside to cool.

Skin and fillet the skate (you will have 6 larger and 6 smaller fillets), reserving the cartilage. Cut the 6 smaller fillets in half to give 12 small, roughly triangular fillets. Place the 6 larger fillets on a work surface, skin-side up, and use 2 small triangular fillets (also skin-side up) to 'patch' each large fillet and make a rectangular shape. Sprinkle with salt and pepper, then divide the mushroom stuffing among the fillets, spreading it over the surface of each rectangle. Roll up into 6 neat cylinders. Spiral 2 slices of pancetta around each cylinder so that they are covered and secured. Stretch open the caul fat as much as possible and tear into 6 pieces large enough to just wrap the cylinders (you may have some left over). Roll cylinders in caul fat, so they are just covered – do not overlap caul fat, as the double layers won't cook through properly. Preheat oven to 220°C.

Meanwhile, make the sauce by melting butter in a saucepan and cooking onion over a medium heat until soft. Add garlic and ginger and cook for 1 minute. Stir in flour and cook for 1–2 minutes, without letting it brown. Stirring constantly, slowly pour in stock, then continue stirring until sauce boils and thickens. Reduce heat and simmer for 10 minutes. Taste, then season with salt and pepper and pass through a fine sieve. Keep warm.

Place skate cylinders on a non-stick baking tray and bake for about 15 minutes, until caul fat is golden brown.

Meanwhile, cut cartilage in half, discarding the thicker part and keeping the thinner, pointed section. Heat vegetable oil in a frying pan and shallow-fry cartilage until golden brown and crisp. Drain on kitchen paper.

Melt remaining butter for stuffing and fry remaining shallots until golden. Add sliced mushrooms and cook until soft. Add salt, pepper and remaining coriander. Keep warm.

To serve, divide mushrooms between 6 plates, top with skate, spoon over sauce and place a piece of fried cartilage on the side.

Braised trout wrapped in sorrel with anchovies + capers

Serves 6

18 large sorrel leaves, thick central rib
    removed
6 × 150 g ocean trout fillets (check for
    bones), skin removed and retained*
1 cup blanched (see page 174), peeled,
    seeded and chopped tomatoes
1½ tablespoons snipped chives
1½ tablespoons chopped flat-leaf
    parsley leaves
1 lemon, thinly sliced
1½ tablespoons small salted capers,
    blanched (see page 174)
12 anchovy fillets (see page 172)
salt, to taste
freshly ground black pepper, to taste
¾ cup extra-virgin olive oil
¾ cup Noilly Prat vermouth
18 boiled small potatoes, to serve

✱ To serve the trout garnished with a bit
of skin, scrape all the scales from the skin,
wash it well, pat it dry, sprinkle with salt
and pepper, and leave on a wire rack in
front of a fan to dry for at least a few
hours, then deep-fry. It bubbles up like
pork crackling.

I'm very fond of this dish, which at MG Garage we used to cook and serve in individual copper pots with Saffron Potatoes (see page 178) on the side. It's an easy dish to make for one person, but just as successful for a crowd. I once served it to 500 people at a Starlight Foundation fund-raising dinner. It's a perfect dish for a large dinner party, as most of the work can be done ahead of time. I often garnish this dish with a crisp deep-fried piece of trout skin.* It's good to start cooking the day before, so that the trout can marinate overnight.

Line 6 moulds (such as Chinese rice bowls or small round take-away containers) with plastic film then with sorrel leaves. Roll each trout fillet up and place in the middle of a mould. Arrange tomatoes, chives, parsley, 2 lemon slices, capers and 2 anchovies around each fillet. Sprinkle with salt and pepper. Fold the sorrel leaves over the fish to enclose and use the plastic film to wrap it into a tight parcel. Refrigerate for a couple of hours, or overnight, for the fish to marinate and for the sorrel leaves to wilt into the shape of the mould.

    Once fish is marinated, preheat oven to 220°C. Take fish parcels out of fridge and leave for 20 minutes to come to room temperature. Unwrap the fish parcels from the plastic film and turn them all out into a baking dish. Pour over olive oil and vermouth and bake for 20 minutes. Remove from oven and leave to rest in baking dish for 5 minutes before serving. Place a fish parcel in the centre of each plate, ladle over the pan juices and pass the potatoes separately.

Rock lobster lettuce rolls with chervil + rock lobster sauce

Serves 6
2 × 500 g green lobsters*
½ cup extra-virgin olive oil
1 small brown onion, chopped
1 clove garlic, chopped
¼ cup brandy*
1 cup dry white wine
500 g tomatoes, chopped
salt, to taste
freshly ground white pepper, to taste
¼ cup picked chervil leaves
chervil leaves, extra, for garnish

Lettuce risotto
2 iceberg lettuce
1 tablespoon oil, retained from above
1 small brown onion, roughly chopped
100 g arborio rice
2 cups hot lobster stock, reserved
    from above
salt, to taste
freshly ground white pepper, to taste

✱ Ask your fishmonger to kill the lobster for you. If you feel confident doing so, flame the brandy before adding it to the sauce. Roasted fennel goes well with this dish.

When I first developed this recipe, I made it with cabbage, but as it was so tiresome making perfect little rolls with the thick cabbage leaves, I moved on to using ordinary iceberg lettuce. This recipe makes the most of the lobster, using the shells for stock and sauce.

Preheat oven to 220°C. Roast lobsters on a baking tray for about 10 minutes, until they just turn red (don't overcook). Allow to cool, then remove all the flesh from the head and the body, and cut into small cubes. Reserve legs for garnish. Place shells in a plastic bag and crush well with a meat mallet or rolling pin. Reserve for the stock and sauce.

Heat oil in a large saucepan and cook onion until soft. Add garlic and crushed shells, and cook for a minute or two. Add brandy and wine, then bring to the boil and cook over a high heat for 1 minute. Add tomatoes, return to boil, then reduce heat, cover and simmer for 20 minutes. Strain through a fine sieve, pressing down on solids to extract as much flavour as possible. Add salt and pepper and set the sauce aside to cool, reserving the solids.

Return solids to the same saucepan, add 3 cups water and bring to the boil for 1 minute. Strain and use this stock for the risotto.

To make the risotto, remove and discard damaged outside leaves from the lettuce and trim off the end of the stem. Remove 9 large, intact leaves and set aside for making the rolls. Weigh remaining lettuce, including the trimmed core – you'll need 200 g, coarsely chopped, for the risotto (use the core and thick stems in preference to the outer leaves). Skim oil off the surface of the sauce, place in a large saucepan and heat. Add onion and fry until golden. Add rice and stir to coat well in oil. Add chopped lettuce and cook for another minute, then add a ladleful of hot stock and stir until almost all is absorbed. Continue adding the stock a ladleful at a time, stirring constantly and allowing each ladleful to be absorbed before adding the next. It will take 20–25 minutes for the risotto to cook. If you run out of stock, use hot water. The risotto should be sloppy, as the lobster meat will absorb some of the liquid. Remove from heat, taste and add salt and pepper. Set aside to cool.

Add lobster and chervil leaves to cooled risotto, check seasoning and refrigerate until cold.

Halve the 9 reserved lettuce leaves, blanch in boiling water until just wilted and refresh in plenty of cold water. Drain well and pat dry. Spread out leaves on work surface and divide the cold risotto mixture among them. Roll up each leaf into a neat parcel. If the leaves are too large, trim off the excess. Steam rolls for 10 minutes.

Spoon lobster sauce onto each of 6 plates and top with 3 lettuce rolls, with extra chervil leaves and reserved lobster legs as a garnish.✱

Barbecued marrons with nettle butter

Serves 6

6 × 500 g (or 12 × 250 g) green marrons
extra-virgin olive oil, for brushing
salt, to taste
freshly ground white pepper, to taste
1 lemon, cut into 6 wedges

Nettle butter

2 bunches (3 firmly packed cups) nettles*
250 g butter
1 teaspoon chopped French tarragon
    leaves (optional)
¼ cup strained lemon juice
salt, to taste
freshly ground white pepper, to taste

✳ When preparing nettles, wear rubber gloves, as any contact with your skin will cause itchiness. Harvested from the wild, only the young shoots and tops of nettles are eaten, but they must be cooked beforehand to remove the stinging element. If nettles are unavailable, use other lemony greens, such as sorrel. If you don't have a barbecue, the marrons can be placed on a baking tray and cooked under a grill.

I first met the late restaurateur Anders Ousback when he was sommelier at Berowra Waters Inn more than 20 years ago. This dish was part of a menu I prepared for Anders' 50th birthday, which included some of his favourite dishes. My last memory of Anders comes from when I visited him the week before he died; he whipped up a pile of pikelets from Margaret Fulton's original cookbook and they became our lunch. Marrons are freshwater crayfish similar to large yabbies (large yabbies or red claws can also be used here), with a moist, firm flesh. They should be sold live, but you can ask your fishmonger to kill them for you – and split them in half lengthwise too. Alternatively, chill them in your freezer until they go to sleep (but don't freeze them), then kill them quickly by chopping them in half lengthwise with one blow from a large, sharp knife.

Start with the nettle butter. Wearing rubber gloves to avoid stings, pick the leaves off the nettles and wash well. Melt 1 tablespoon of the butter in a small saucepan, add nettles and cook for 1 minute, until thoroughly wilted (the sting disappears from nettles once they're cooked). Squeeze nettles well to remove excess liquid, then chop very finely. You should end up with about 6 tablespoons chopped nettles.

Cut each marron in half lengthwise. Brush shell and flesh liberally with oil, then season flesh with salt and pepper. Heat a barbecue or a chargrill pan* and grill marrons, shell-side down for a few minutes, until shell turns red. Turn and cook flesh side for about 1 minute, until just cooked (bearing in mind that they will continue to cook in the residual heat once you take them off the barbecue).

Meanwhile, finish nettle butter by heating remaining butter in a frying pan and cooking until it just starts to turn brown – watch it closely so that it doesn't foam over the sides of the pan and catch fire. Add nettles and allow to sizzle for a minute, taking care not to burn them. Add tarragon (if using) and lemon juice. Bring to the boil then remove from heat and add salt and pepper.

Place marrons, flesh-side up, on 6 plates, pour over nettle butter and serve with lemon wedges.

Braised then grilled octopus with broad beans + braised then grilled red onions

Serves 6
12 × 250 g octopus
3 cloves garlic, chopped
3 sprigs flat-leaf parsley, chopped
1 teaspoon chopped oregano leaves
freshly ground black pepper, to taste
grated zest of 1 lemon
1 cup extra-virgin olive oil
1 cup Roast Tomato Sauce (see page 178)
pinch dried Greek oregano (see page 172)
1 tablespoon extra-virgin olive oil, extra
3 kg broad beans, shelled, blanched
    (see page 174) and skinned

Braised then grilled red onions
2 large red onions
¼ cup extra-virgin olive oil
¼ cup dry white wine
salt, to taste
freshly ground black pepper, to taste

✸ This dish is great served with Saffron Potatoes (see page 178).

I prefer larger octopus to the baby ones that seem so popular on menus today. I don't remember eating baby octopus in Greece – it was always large octopus, which the fishermen beat against the rocks to tenderise, then spread over a clothes line to dry a little before grilling. As you pass by tavernas all along the coast of Greece, you can smell the distinctive aroma of sun-dried octopus being grilled. Braising the octopus before grilling makes it tender and gives it plenty of flavour. I developed this method because I was tired of eating the little rubbery octopus that had just been quickly tossed on a grill.

Preheat oven to 175°C. Cut heads off octopus and discard (or retain for another dish), then remove beaks (the hard piece of cartilage in the centre of the legs). Pack octopus tightly into a baking dish, then sprinkle with garlic, parsley, oregano leaves, pepper, lemon zest and half the 1 cup olive oil. Place dampened baking paper over the dish, pressing it down onto the surface of the octopus. Cover the dish tightly with foil or a lid and place in oven. After 1 hour, turn the octopus over, making sure it's submerged in the liquid. Continue cooking until tender to the bite – this may take another half to 1 hour. When octopus is cooked, remove from oven, leave to cool in liquid, then refrigerate.

Meanwhile, start grilled red onions by cutting onions into 6 mm slices. Place in a baking dish just large enough to hold them in a single layer. Drizzle with olive oil and white wine, sprinkle with salt and pepper, and place dampened baking paper over the top, pressing it down onto the surface of the onions. Cover the dish tightly with foil or a lid. Bake onions until soft, about 45 minutes. Remove from oven and allow to cool completely in liquid.

Pour 1 cup octopus liquid into a saucepan. Boil until reduced by half then add Roast Tomato Sauce, oregano and remaining ½ cup olive oil. Taste and adjust seasoning.

Heat extra 1 tablespoon olive oil in a frying pan and toss broad beans to warm them through. Keep warm.

Heat a chargrill plate or barbecue, and grill octopus and onions until warmed through and a little charred. Serve with sauce and broad beans.

Braised stuffed squid

Serves 6

1.5 kg small squid
3 tablespoons light olive oil
1 small brown onion, chopped
2 tablespoons plain flour
1 clove garlic, chopped
1 cup dry white wine
1 cup hot water
1 dried bay leaf
salt, to taste
freshly ground black pepper, to taste
½ cup torn basil leaves, to serve
cooked polenta (see page 90), Handmade
    Sicilian-style Macaroni (see page 177)
    or short pasta, to serve

Stuffing

500 g tomatoes
100 ml light olive oil
1 large brown onion, chopped
2 teaspoons tomato paste
3 cloves garlic, chopped
150 g Toasted Herb Breadcrumbs
    (see page 175)
3 tablespoons chopped flat-leaf
    parsley leaves
3 egg yolks, lightly beaten
salt, to taste
freshly ground black pepper, to taste

Tomato squid sauce

1 cup dry white wine
1 cup Roast Tomato Sauce (see page 178)
½ cup extra-virgin olive oil
salt, to taste
freshly ground black pepper, to taste
squid cooking liquid, reserved from above

Not all pasta comes from a pasta machine; this dish can be served with Handmade Sicilian-style Macaroni. I was surprised one day when an MG Garage apprentice, Joe Gambacorta, told me how his mum made her macaroni at home, rolling each individual macarono around a knitting needle. Excited by the idea of learning something new, I asked his mum to come and show us. It was such a fun day, and we put the macaroni on the menu with the braised squid.

Clean (but don't peel) squid, chop tentacles and set aside for stuffing.

To make the stuffing, blanch the tomatoes (see page 174), then peel, seed and chop them, reserving and straining the juices. Heat oil in a saucepan or frying pan and fry onion until brown. Add tomatoes, reserved tomato juice, tomato paste and garlic, then cook until thick. Allow to cool, then add breadcrumbs, parsley, egg yolks, salt and pepper, and reserved chopped tentacles.

Stuff squid tubes without overfilling. Pack filled tubes tightly into a baking dish, in a single layer, head to tail so the mixture won't spill out as it cooks.

Preheat oven to 150°C. Heat olive oil in a saucepan and fry onion until it browns. Sprinkle with flour and cook, stirring for a minute. Add garlic, wine, water and bay leaf, then bring to the boil, reduce heat and simmer for 10 minutes. Taste, add salt and pepper, and pour over squid. Cover with dampened baking paper, pressing down onto the surface of the squid. Bake for 1–1½ hours, until a skewer easily goes through the squid.

When squid is cooked, carefully remove squid tubes from the baking dish and keep warm. Make the tomato squid sauce by adding wine, Roast Tomato Sauce, olive oil, salt and pepper to the baking dish with the squid cooking liquid and stirring to combine. Bring to the boil then remove from heat.

Return squid to the baking dish to serve, and scatter with basil leaves. Serve with polenta, Handmade Sicilian-style Macaroni or pasta.

Confit of ~~boned~~ duck with a duck gizzard + curly endive salad

Serves 6

3 × 1.6 kg ducks, boned and halved
    lengthwise*
3 cloves garlic, chopped
1½ tablespoons thyme leaves
6 dried bay leaves, crumbled
freshly grated nutmeg, to taste
freshly ground black pepper, to taste
salt, to taste
6 × 25 cm squares muslin
kitchen twine
700 g tinned duck or goose fat*
½ cup water

Duck gizzard & curly endive salad

500 g duck or chicken gizzards*
salt, to taste
freshly ground black pepper, to taste
1 cup water
1 cup duck or goose fat, reserved
    from above
1 bunch curly endive
1 tablespoon duck or goose fat, extra,
    reserved from above
¼ cup red wine vinegar

✳ Your butcher or poultry supplier
will bone and halve the ducks for you,
and supply duck or chicken gizzards.
Tinned duck or goose fat is available in
delicatessens and specialty food shops.
If you can't find it, combine 1 kg minced
pork fat (from a butcher) with 1 cup water
in a saucepan, simmer over a very low heat
for 2 hours until the fat separates from the
golden solids (taking care not to burn the
fat), then strain and discard the solids.

This dish needs to be made a few days in advance for the flavours to develop. The French traditionally store a confit under fat to preserve it, and it is considered to improve with age. A classic confit of duck should taste salty and garlicky. Remember, when dealing with fat, one should always beware of fire. One wonderful cook and dear friend once burned down a commercial kitchen cooking confit of duck. If boning and rolling ducks seems too fiddly, use 6 large duck legs instead of 3 whole ducks.

At least 2 days before serving, lay duck halves on a plate or baking tray, skin-side down, scatter over chopped garlic, thyme leaves and crumbled bay leaves, and sprinkle over nutmeg, pepper and generous amounts of salt. Cover tray with plastic film, pressing it down onto the surface of the ducks, and refrigerate overnight.

The next day, preheat oven to 175°C. Roll each duck half from head to toe into a fat sausage shape about 5 × 12 cm. Wrap each roll in a muslin square, secure well with plenty of kitchen twine and place in a small, deep-sided baking dish or pan in which the rolls fit tightly and that has a lid. Combine duck or goose fat and water in a small saucepan over a low heat. Pour over duck sausages, completely covering them. Place baking dish on stove top and heat until liquid just starts to simmer. Remove from heat, cover with dampened baking paper, then very tightly with foil, sealing well, and then with the lid, and bake for 2 hours. Check that the liquid has not changed colour and isn't sizzling – the water mixed in with the fat should prevent this from happening, but if the dish hasn't been properly sealed the water may have evaporated and the ducks will be frying in the oil rather than poaching. If this has happened, they are cooked by now and shouldn't be returned to the oven. If all is well, reseal and return to oven for another hour, checking again after 30 minutes.

Remove cooked ducks from the oven and set aside to cool in the fat. When they are cool, but the fat is still liquid, transfer ducks to a container large enough to just hold them, and pour over just enough fat to cover well. Refrigerate until the day of serving. Strain and refrigerate just over 1 cup excess duck fat for cooking gizzards.

On the day before serving, start the salad by splitting the gizzards, washing them well and sprinkling them with salt and pepper. Place gizzards, with water and reserved fat, in a frying pan that has a lid. Bring to the boil, then reduce heat and simmer, covered tightly, for about 1 hour (for chicken gizzards) or 2 hours (for large duck gizzards), watching carefully to make sure the water isn't evaporating (as with ducks above). The gizzards will be cooked when a skewer passes through them easily. Cool, then pour gizzards and fat into a small container, cover and refrigerate.➜

The next day (the day of serving), preheat oven to 220°C. Remove duck sausages from fat, remove and discard muslin, then place sausages on a non-stick baking tray and bake for about 20 minutes until crisp.

Meanwhile finish salad by washing and drying endive and placing in a salad bowl. Remove gizzards from fat, trim away the tough skin and, if using duck gizzards, slice thinly (chicken gizzards are smaller and can be left whole). Heat extra duck or goose fat in a frying pan over a medium heat and fry gizzards until they sizzle and become slightly crisp. Add vinegar and cook until it bubbles, then pour the lot over the endive. Season with salt and pepper, toss well and serve with the crisp confit.

What is a confit?

Traditionally confit refers to cooking meat in fat over a low heat until much of the meat's moisture is replaced by the fat. The meat is then stored covered with this fat to preserve it. Many modern recipes and menus use the word 'confit' in reference to vegetables, meaning that the vegetable has been immersed in olive oil (or fat, often goose or duck fat) and cooked over a low heat until it has absorbed a lot of the oil and its flavour. While this gives a lovely rich texture, it does not preserve the vegetables in the same way as a traditional confit preserves meat.

Using leftovers

Strain and refrigerate excess duck fat from this recipe and use it for frying potatoes. Potatoes fried in duck fat make an excellent accompaniment to this dish, as do homemade baked beans. Confit of duck can be shredded while hot into a bitter leaf salad, and I have also mixed it with duck liver and apple to make a rich stuffing for cabbage rolls.

Spatchcock baked in salt crust with parsley sauce

Serves 6
6 × 500 g spatchcocks
1 firmly packed tablespoon thyme leaves
1 lemon, sliced
freshly ground white pepper, to taste
125 g butter, very well softened

Salt crust
1.5 kg baker's flour
1.5 kg salt*
1 litre water

Parsley sauce
150 g flat-leaf parsley leaves
600 ml 35%-fat cream
salt, to taste
freshly ground white pepper, to taste

✱ You can use regular cooking salt for the dough. If you find the spatchcocks a bit too salty, place a small square of baking paper under each bird before wrapping it in the salt crust.

I once cooked these spatchcocks when we were invited for a day out on a friend's boat on Sydney Harbour with Stephanie Alexander, and Damien and Josephine Pignolet. We arrived with a basketful of salt-crust spatchcocks and salad and several bottles of champagne, only to realise the boat was a small catamaran. The spatchcocks and salad were devoured, but the champagne was hardly touched due to the absence of a toilet on the little boat! You need to make the dough for the salt crust the day before and leave it overnight so that it becomes more pliable.

The day before, make the salt crust. Combine flour and salt, add water and knead until you have a firm dough. Cover and leave to rest at room temperature overnight.

The next day, preheat oven to 220°C. Cut dough into 6 portions and roll each portion on a floured surface into a circle large enough to encase a spatchcock, about 35 cm diameter. Leave a slightly thicker section in the centre of each circle (to help hold the dough together and protect the breast).

Wash spatchcocks well, inside and out, and dry on kitchen paper. Place half the thyme leaves, a lemon slice and a good grinding of white pepper in the cavity of each spatchcock and rub them in well. Brush the outside of each bird liberally with softened butter, sprinkle over remaining thyme leaves, and place each bird, breast down, in the centre of a dough circle. Wrap and smooth dough around the birds well, gathering the dough together and enclosing them completely. Place on 1 or 2 baking trays, breast up (securing the dough well underneath the birds), and bake for about 40 minutes, until the dough turns golden brown. The best way to test the spatchcock is cooked is to push a thin metal skewer through the pastry into the thigh and then test the skewer against your lower lip – it should feel hot.

To make the sauce, add parsley to a large saucepan of boiling water and boil for a couple of minutes, until quite soft. Drain parsley and squeeze well. Bring cream to the boil and, watching it carefully so it doesn't boil over, cook for a couple of minutes until reduced by a third. Add parsley and return to the boil. Carefully purée in a blender (remember it's hot), pass through a fine sieve and add salt and pepper. Keep warm.

Using a serrated knife, very carefully cut around the centre of the pastry, being careful not to cut the spatchcock. Lift each spatchcock out of its crust and onto a plate and pour over parsley sauce.

Alternatively, you can serve the spatchcocks in their crusts for guests to remove at the table, remembering they'll need to dispose of the crust – which is definitely not edible. The guests can then help themselves to parsley sauce.

Guinea fowl baked in clay with pancetta, mushrooms + barley pilaf

Serves 6

6 large field mushrooms
60 g butter
1 teaspoon thyme leaves
1 tablespoon chopped flat-leaf parsley
    leaves
salt, to taste
freshly ground white pepper, to taste
3 × 1.2 kg guinea fowl
1½ tablespoons brandy
kitchen twine
18 thin slices flat pancetta
6 leaves iceberg lettuce
125 g butter, melted
3 × 500 g blocks clay*
plain flour, for rolling clay

Barley pilaf

125 g butter
1 medium brown onion, chopped
1 cup pearl barley
4 cups water
½ teaspoon cumin seeds, toasted
    (see page 174)
1 cup currants
2 teaspoons salt
1 teaspoon freshly ground black pepper
1 tablespoon strained lemon juice
grated zest of 1 lemon

✱ Clay is available in art supply shops.
For a richer sauce, pour 2 tablespoons hot
Veal Glaze (see page 176) over each bird
before serving.

As guinea fowl are generally dry birds, enclosing them in clay ensures they cook evenly in their own steam and remain moist. Encasing food is one of the signatures of my cooking. I use any possible way to make sure the food remains moist and retains its flavour, and I love the theatre of unwrapping the parcels. Start this recipe the day before, for the flavour of the pancetta to marry with the bird overnight and give a nice rosy colour to the breast.

The day before, wipe mushrooms with a damp cloth and trim off the stalks. Slice mushrooms thinly. Melt the 60 g butter in a frying pan and cook mushrooms until soft. Add thyme, parsley, salt and pepper. Set aside to cool.

Remove head, neck, wing tips and feet from guinea fowl (keep these for a game stock – follow Chicken Stock recipe on page 176). Wash birds inside and out and dry well. Place salt, pepper and 2 teaspoons brandy in the cavity of each bird. Divide cooled mushrooms among the cavities. Tie the ends of the legs around the tail with kitchen twine. Cover each breast with 6 pancetta slices. Blanch iceberg lettuce leaves in boiling water until pliable, refresh in cold water, dry, then drape 2 leaves over each breast. Brush each bird liberally with the melted butter. Lay 2 × 50 cm long sheets of baking paper on a bench, overlapping them as much as possible, but so the bird will be enclosed completely with an overlap of 3 cm at the top. Place a bird on the paper, breast up, and wrap up, folding all the ends together to make a secure parcel. Repeat with remaining birds. Place a block of clay on a lightly floured bench, sprinkle with flour and roll into a 40 cm square. Place one baking paper parcel onto the square of clay on the diagonal, breast down. Fold corners up to the centre of the parcel and pat down gently to seal. Repeat with the remaining guinea fowl and clay. Refrigerate overnight.

The next day, preheat oven to 150°C. Make the barley pilaf by melting butter in an ovenproof saucepan or a small baking dish, preferably with a lid. Add onion and fry over a medium heat until golden brown. Add barley and stir for a minute. Add water, cumin seeds, currants, salt and pepper. Cover with lid, or seal well with foil, and bake for 1½ hours. Stir through lemon juice and zest and keep warm. Increase oven to 220°C.

Once oven is up to temperature, place clay parcels on a baking tray and bake for 50 minutes. Remove from oven and leave to rest for 10 minutes.

Break the top of the clay parcels and open them out. Roll the baking paper down to partially unwrap the birds. Transfer each bird to a chopping board and remove stuffing, returning stuffing to the baking paper-lined clay vessel. Cut off legs and carve breast, and place on top of the stuffing. Place clay vessels on a long serving platter and take to the table with a bowl of barley pilaf to pass separately.

Quail bisteeya

Serves 6

6 × 200 g quails
2 cloves garlic, chopped
1½ teaspoons salt
1 teaspoon freshly ground black pepper
3 sprigs flat-leaf parsley, chopped
3 teaspoons chopped coriander leaves
1 small brown onion, chopped
¼ teaspoon ground turmeric
½ teaspoon ground ginger
1 cinnamon stick, crushed
80 g butter
1 cup water
2 tablespoons plain flour
¼ cup strained lemon juice
5 eggs, lightly beaten
6 × 60 cm strips Greek Filo Pastry*
    (see page 177)
250 g butter, melted
3 tablespoons pure icing sugar
1 teaspoon ground cinnamon

Almonds

150 g whole almonds, blanched and
    toasted (see page 174)
1½ teaspoons pure icing sugar
¾ teaspoon ground cinnamon
¾ teaspoon ground cayenne pepper
1–2 drops almond essence (optional)

Fig, pomegranate & witlof salad

1 large pomegranate
extra-virgin olive oil, for dressing
3 Corella pears
6 small heads white or pink witlof,
    leaves separated
3 golden shallots, sliced
salt, to taste
freshly ground black pepper, to taste
6 figs, quartered

✳ You'll need 1½ quantities of my Greek
Filo Pastry. If you use bought filo, you'll
need to use a double thickness.

The Moroccan dish on which this recipe is based traditionally uses pigeon and is made as one large pie. It is also traditionally made with warka pastry, but I have adapted it for my Greek filo pastry. In her fantastic book on Moroccan cooking, Paula Wolfert discusses bisteeyas in great detail, describing the traditional method women use to make warka pastry. I have tried to make it a few times but failed spectacularly each time. One could argue that my version is not a true bisteeya, but I think it would be wrong of me to give it any other name when it is so heavily based on the traditional recipe. I can't very well call it 'Janni's pie'!

Pack quails tightly into a saucepan large enough to just hold them in a single layer. Combine garlic, salt and pepper, parsley sprigs, coriander, onion, turmeric, ginger and cinnamon stick, and pack around the quail. Dot butter on top and pour over water. Bring to a boil, reduce heat and simmer, covered, for 10 minutes. Set aside to cool.

Remove meat from bones and chop into thick chunks. Skim butter off cooking liquid and place in a saucepan. Strain cooking liquid and set aside. Mix flour into skimmed-off butter and cook over a medium heat until lightly browned. Add cooking liquid and stir constantly over a low heat until sauce thickens. Add lemon juice and eggs and stir until the eggs separate into thick curds. Add quail meat, and adjust seasoning if required.

Coarsely grind the almonds in a food processor and mix with the other ingredients.

Preheat oven to 200°C. Lay a sheet of pastry on a clean, dry work surface (keep remaining sheets covered to prevent them drying out). Brush pastry liberally with melted butter and put one-sixth of the quail mixture on one corner of the pastry. Carefully fold the corner with the filling over to make a triangle, then continue to fold triangle until almost all of the pastry strip is used. Before the final fold, brush triangle with melted butter, sprinkle over 1½ tablespoons almond mixture, then make final fold and tuck any remaining pastry under to secure the pie. Liberally butter the top of the pie and place on a baking tray. Repeat with remaining pastry and quail mixture. Bake for about 10 minutes, until golden.

Meanwhile, make the salad. Seed the pomegranate, reserving ⅓ cup of the seeds for the salad. Place the rest in a sieve over a bowl and press down with a pestle to extract as much juice as possible. Discard solids. Combine pomegranate juice with an equal quantity of extra-virgin olive oil. Core and thinly slice pears and place in a bowl. Add witlof, shallots, reserved pomegranate seeds, combined juice and olive oil, salt and pepper. Toss gently and transfer to a serving platter. Arrange figs on top of the salad.

Sift a little icing sugar over the cooked pies and make a decorative line down the centre of each pie with a pinch of ground cinnamon.

Roast squab with heart + liver cabbage rolls

Serves 6

6 × 500 g squabs
salt, to taste
freshly ground black pepper, to taste
extra-virgin olive oil, for coating birds

Squab stock

trimmings from squabs (neck, wings
    and feet), reserved from above
1 small brown onion, chopped
1 small carrot, chopped
½ stick celery, chopped
2 cloves garlic
2 cups water or Chicken Stock
    (see page 176)

Cabbage rolls

hearts and livers from squabs, reserved
    from above
100 g butter
1 tablespoon brandy
½ cup Fresh Breadcrumbs (see page 175)
1 small brown onion, chopped
100 g bacon, diced
1 clove garlic, chopped
150 g green cabbage, chopped
2 tablespoons chopped flat-leaf
    parsley leaves
½ teaspoon thyme leaves
salt, to taste
freshly ground black pepper, to taste
6 green cabbage leaves, halved

Sauce

¼ cup brandy
1 cup dry red wine
1½ cups hot squab stock, reserved
    from above
4 strips orange zest
pinch crushed juniper berries
salt, to taste
freshly ground black pepper, to taste
2 tablespoons cold butter, cubed

Autumn days, with the increasing chill in the air, turn my thoughts to game. This dish is one of my favourite ways of serving squab (young pigeon). In Australia we don't have regional cuisines as in other countries – our region is the whole world. But our produce comes from different areas, and when I first made this dish, I used squab from the Glenloth Game farm in north-western Victoria. For a lighter version, use iceberg lettuce instead of cabbage leaves. If squab livers and hearts aren't available, substitute chicken livers.

Remove the insides of the squabs and reserve the hearts and livers for the cabbage roll stuffing. Cut off the neck, wings and feet and reserve for the stock. Rinse squabs (inside and out) and trimmings and pat dry. Refrigerate.

To make the stock, preheat oven to 200°C. Roast the reserved squab trimmings with the onion, carrot, celery and garlic in a greased baking dish until brown, about 15 minutes. Place baking dish on the stove top, add the water or stock, and cook until the bits crusted onto the bottom of the pan come off. Pour the mixture into a small saucepan, cover, and simmer for about 1 hour. Strain through a fine sieve, discarding solids. Keep 1½ cups hot, for making the sauce.

Meanwhile, make the cabbage rolls by cutting the reserved hearts and livers into small cubes. Melt 20 g of the butter in a frying pan, add hearts and livers and fry over a medium heat for a couple of minutes. Add brandy and stir for a minute to remove the bits crusted onto the bottom of the pan. Remove from the pan and set aside. In the same pan, melt another 20 g butter and fry breadcrumbs until golden. Remove from pan. Melt remaining butter in the same pan and cook the onion and bacon over a medium heat until soft but not browned. Add the garlic and chopped cabbage and continue cooking until the cabbage is tender. Remove from pan and combine with hearts and livers, breadcrumbs, herbs, salt and pepper.

Blanch the halved cabbage leaves in boiling water for 1 minute, then refresh in plenty of cold water. Discard the tough stem sections and lay the cabbage leaves out flat. Divide stuffing into 12 portions, place a portion of stuffing on each leaf half then roll up to form cabbage rolls. Cover and set aside at room temperature (refrigerate if making rolls well ahead of time).

Increase oven temperature to 250°C. Remove squabs from fridge and leave for 20 minutes to come to room temperature. Season squabs, inside and out, with salt and pepper, and rub skin with olive oil. Place in a greased baking dish and bake for about 15 minutes, until golden brown – the breasts should remain pink. Remove cooked squabs from dish and leave in a warm place for 10 minutes. Discard fat but don't wash dish.➜

Kid + kibbeh pies with barberry sauce + spinach

Serves 8

plain flour, for dusting
125 g butter
800 g baby spinach
freshly grated nutmeg, to taste
salt, to taste
freshly ground black pepper, to taste

Braised kid

600 g kid meat from 1 long leg,
    cut into walnut-sized pieces
1 tablespoon plain flour
salt, to taste
1 tablespoon Ras El Hanout (see page 177)
120 g butter
1 medium brown onion, cut into 8 wedges
1 medium carrot, sliced
½ small stick celery, sliced
1 medium turnip, cut into 8 wedges
8 cloves garlic, peeled
300 ml Chicken Stock (see page 176)

Kibbeh

200 g fine cracked wheat (burghul)
500 g very lean, sinew-free lamb, minced
1 large brown onion, finely chopped
1½ bird's-eye chillies, deseeded and
    chopped
2 teaspoons salt
2 teaspoons cumin seeds, ground
2 teaspoons allspice, ground

Barberry sauce

1 litre kid stock or Veal Stock (see page 176)
80 g cold butter, cubed
4 golden shallots, sliced
½ cup dried barberries*
salt, to taste
pinch Ras El Hanout (see page 177)

✱ Barberries are available in Middle
Eastern delicatessens, or you could use
sumac or grated lemon zest. Make 1 large
pie by putting kid mixture into a baking
dish with a layer of kibbeh on top.

Here is another engineering feat. I'm sorry, I can't help it – it must be my background that keeps me fascinated with the technical aspects of cooking. For some time I had an idea of enclosing a pie filling in another meat mixture instead of pastry, and in this recipe it's been realised. It was well worth the effort! You need to start this recipe the day before, or at least the morning before, as the braised kid needs to become cold and solidify before it's used as the pie filling.

The day before, make the braised kid. Preheat oven to 175°C. Toss the kid in the combined flour, salt and Ras El Hanout in a bowl. Melt half the butter in a frying pan then brown the kid. Remove from pan and set aside. Melt remaining butter in the same pan and brown the onion, carrot, celery and turnip. Place meat, vegetables and garlic cloves in a baking dish that can be used on the stove top and that has a lid. Add stock, bring just to the boil, remove from heat and cover with dampened baking paper, pressing it down onto the surface of the meat. Cover tightly with foil and the lid. Bake for 1½ hours.

Remove from oven and allow to cool in cooking liquid. Strain off cooking liquid, being careful to avoid crushing the vegetables. Set solids aside and leave liquid to rest for a few minutes until the fat rises to the surface. Skim off and discard as much fat as possible. Pour skimmed cooking liquid over the meat and vegetables and refrigerate overnight to set.

To make the kibbeh, soak the cracked wheat in cold water for 5 minutes, then squeeze dry in a tea towel and set aside. Process lamb, onion, chillies, salt, ground cumin and ground allspice in a food processor until very well combined. Add cracked wheat and process until just combined. Seal tightly in a plastic bag to prevent the meat from oxidising and refrigerate overnight.

The next day, divide kibbeh into 8 pieces, cover and return to the fridge. Divide cold kid and vegetable mixture into 8 portions. Shape into 8 balls, wrap tightly in plastic film to retain their shape and return to refrigerator.

Preheat oven to 250°C. Lay a sheet of plastic film on a work surface and dust well with flour. Place one portion of kibbeh on the plastic film and pat into a circle, then dust well with flour, place another sheet of plastic film on top and, using a rolling pin, roll into a circle large enough (15–20 cm) to enclose a ball of kid mixture. Remove top piece of plastic film and lift the kibbeh, on the bottom sheet of plastic film, into a Chinese soup bowl (or similar vessel). Place a ball of kid mixture in the centre of the kibbeh and wrap kibbeh over the top, pressing gently to seal the parcel well. Cut a 15 cm square of baking paper, place on top of the pie and turn pie out onto baking paper. Remove plastic film.➜

Poke a skewer in the top of the pie to make a hole for steam to escape, and score the top of the pie, in curves from the central hole, using the tip of a knife, to make it look a little like puff pastry. Place pie on a baking tray and refrigerate. Repeat with remaining mixture.

Bake pies for 15–20 minutes, until brown, remembering that the inside of the pie is already cooked and so only needs to be heated through.

Meanwhile, make barberry sauce by pouring stock into a small saucepan and boiling until reduced by half. Set aside. Melt half the butter in a saucepan and fry shallots until golden, then add barberries and cook for another minute. Add reduced stock, bring to the boil, reduce heat and simmer for 5 minutes. Add salt and Ras El Hanout. Whisk in remaining butter, piece by piece.

To prepare the spinach, melt butter in a wok, add spinach and toss until wilted. Sprinkle with nutmeg, salt and pepper and keep warm.

Serve pies with wilted spinach on the side and barberry sauce spooned over.

Things to do with kid and kibbeh

You can serve braised kid as a dish in its own right: combine it with some stock, taste it and correct the seasoning. Serve it with your favourite vegetables and polenta, couscous or steamed potatoes.

Kibbeh is delicious served raw on toast or Lebanese bread with a drop of olive oil as an appetiser. Or try wrapping it around skewers and grilling, or shaping it into patties and pan-frying or deep-frying.

Seared venison fillet with cabbage + beetroot purée

Serves 6

2 × 600 g venison fillets
3 tablespoons coarsely ground
    black pepper
3 tablespoons coarsely ground
    juniper berries
light olive oil, to cover

Beetroot purée

700 g beetroot
2 tablespoons extra-virgin olive oil
1 medium brown onion, chopped
1 clove garlic, chopped
1½ tablespoons balsamic vinegar
1 cup Roast Tomato Sauce (see page 178)
¼ cup Veal Glaze (see page 176) (optional)
¼ cup water
salt, to taste
freshly ground black pepper, to taste
1 tablespoon 35%-fat cream

Braised red cabbage

100 g butter
2 medium red onions, chopped
1 teaspoon brown sugar
3 teaspoons red wine vinegar
1 cup dry red wine
300 g red cabbage, shredded
pinch crushed juniper berries
salt, to taste
freshly ground black pepper, to taste

Venison sauce

2 tablespoons cold butter
venison trimmings, reserved from above
1 cup dry red wine
1 cup Veal Glaze (see page 176)
pinch crushed juniper berries
salt, to taste
freshly ground black pepper, to taste

✱ The purée and cabbage can be made the day before and reheated when needed.

I have also made this dish using kangaroo, wallaby and even hare fillets. Australian cuisine has been very slow to make use of indigenous produce; we've only been eating kangaroo meat in the last few years. In 1996 I unwittingly created quite a stir by putting possum on the menu at Bennelong. People were outraged that I would serve one of our native animals on a dinner plate. In fact, some of the Opera House staff circulated leaflets among themselves calling for a boycott of Bennelong . . . I wonder if they ever relished eating local game when holidaying in Europe. You'll need to start marinating the venison the day before.

The day before, trim all sinew from the fillets and set trimmings aside for venison sauce. Roll fillets in combined pepper and juniper berries. Place in a small dish in a single layer and cover with olive oil. Refrigerate overnight.

Steam beetroot for 1–2 hours (depending on their size), until a skewer passes through them easily. Peel while still hot and slice thickly. Refrigerate overnight.

The next day, make the beetroot purée by heating oil in a large frying pan and cooking onion and garlic until soft. Add vinegar and heat until it bubbles. Add beetroot, Roast Tomato Sauce, Veal Glaze (if using), water, salt and pepper, and cook over a low heat for about 1 hour, stirring occasionally, until most of the liquid has evaporated. Combine with cream in a blender to make a very smooth purée. Keep warm.

To prepare the red cabbage, in a large frying pan that has a lid, heat butter until foaming and fry onions until golden. Add sugar, vinegar, wine and cabbage, and cook, covered, over a low heat for about 1 hour, until soft. Remove lid, increase heat and continue to cook, stirring, until most of the liquid has evaporated. Add juniper berries, salt and pepper. Keep warm.

Heat a barbecue plate or heavy-based frying pan until very hot. Remove fillets from olive oil and sear them quickly on each side, so they remain very rare inside. Remove from barbecue or pan and rest in a warm place.

Meanwhile, make sauce by melting half the butter in a frying pan and cooking venison trimmings until well browned. Add wine and cook over a low heat until liquid is reduced by half. Add Veal Glaze and heat through, then add juniper berries, salt and pepper. Pass through a fine sieve into a clean saucepan and, over a medium heat, whisk in remaining butter. Keep warm.

To serve, cut each venison fillet into 15 slices, on the diagonal (follow the grain of the meat with your knife for smooth slices). Place 1 tablespoon red cabbage on each plate, then top with 5 slices venison and a scoop of beetroot purée. Pour sauce over meat.

Braised then fried pork hock with kumara purée + Cumberland sauce

Serves 6

3 × 650 g boned pork hocks
1 tablespoon salt
2¼ teaspoons Quatre Épices (see page 178)
3 large pieces muslin
kitchen twine
3 cloves garlic, peeled
1 cup dry white wine
6 thin slices ginger
3 dried bay leaves
3 sprigs thyme
vegetable oil, for deep-frying

Cumberland sauce

4 tablespoons finely chopped spring
    onions
zest of 1 orange, cut into thin strips and
    blanched (see page 174)
zest of 1 lemon, cut into thin strips and
    blanched (see page 174)
2 cm cube ginger, cut into thin strips
⅔ cup tawny port
⅓ cup strained orange juice
2½ tablespoons strained lemon juice
170 g redcurrant jelly
pinch cayenne pepper
salt, to taste
freshly ground white pepper, to taste

Kumara purée

1.5 kg kumara
125 g butter
grated zest of 1 orange
salt, to taste
freshly ground white pepper, to taste
½ cup strained orange juice
1 cup 35%-fat cream

When I cook with pork, I often use the extremities, such as the ears and hocks, or the offal. One year for the 'Hats Off' dinner, however, I decided to create a festive menu based around roasted whole suckling pigs. We called it 'Carnevale Veneziano' and as the guests arrived they all received a colourful Venetian-style mask to wear. The menu started with antipasto and carpaccio, included risotto nero and finished with a Bellini Sorbet (see page 143). I wanted to create a theatrical experience for our guests at MG Garage that night, so the whole pigs were roasted next door in Fuel's baker's ovens. When it was time to serve, the waiters quickly set up a carving area in the middle of the restaurant and the chefs each paraded a whole suckling pig on its platter through the restaurant before placing it on the carving table, where it was chopped into chunks and sent to the tables on large platters. I remember the amusement of some guests, and the dismay of others, when my enthusiastic performance sent a pig's head rolling down the middle of the restaurant! You need to start this recipe the day before, to prepare the hocks.

The day before, lay hock meat on a chopping board skin-side down and sprinkle over salt and Quatre Épices. Roll each hock into a sausage shape, with the skin on the outside, then wrap in muslin and tie with plenty of twine to maintain the sausage shape. Place hocks in a saucepan or braising pan in which they fit snugly. Add garlic, white wine, ginger, bay leaves and thyme. Cover with a tight-fitting lid, bring to the boil, reduce heat to very low, then simmer for 3–4 hours, turning the hocks every now and then and checking that the liquid hasn't evaporated before the meat is cooked. If liquid evaporates too soon, reduce heat and add a little boiling water. Remove cooked hocks from the pan and refrigerate until completely cold.

The next day, make Cumberland sauce. Combine all ingredients in a saucepan, bring to the boil, reduce heat to a simmer and cook until reduced to 1 cup. Refrigerate until cold. If it becomes too thick when cold, dilute with a little hot water to serve.

Meanwhile, steam whole kumara, in their skin, for about 45 minutes, until a skewer passes through them easily. As soon as they are cool enough to handle, peel and pass through a sieve into a mixing bowl. Add butter, orange zest, salt and pepper, and mix well. Add three-quarters of the orange juice and cream, and mix well. If consistency is as desired, leave purée as is; if too thick, add enough of the remaining orange juice and cream to form a light purée. Keep warm.

Remove the twine and muslin from the hocks, wipe off any jelly, and cut each one into 4 pieces. Heat oil in a deep-sided, preferably non-stick saucepan and deep-fry hock →

pieces in batches for about 10 minutes, until skin is crisp. (Avoid overcrowding the pan, or the hock pieces may stick together and the oil may lose too much heat. Be careful as you cook the hock pieces, as the meat will spit as it cooks. You can protect yourself by placing a spatter guard or an upside-down sieve on top of the saucepan.) Drain on kitchen paper. Keep fried pieces warm in a low oven.

Place 2 pieces of hock on each plate, spoon over Cumberland sauce, and serve kumara purée on the side.

Asian inspiration

This dish was inspired by the deep-fried whole pork hocks of Asian cooking, where the final deep-frying occurs in a wok (which you could also use for this recipe), but I've adapted the Asian technique by first boning the hocks. Kumara chips are also good with this dish. For a buffet or a picnic, serve thin slices of the pork cold with cornichons or Cumberland sauce.

Bacon + herb crumbed fillet of rabbit with rabbit liver faggots

Serves 6

3 × 1.5 kg farmed rabbits*
½ cup Toasted Herb Breadcrumbs
    (see page 175)
¼ cup very finely diced bacon
¼ cup chopped flat-leaf parsley leaves
½ cup plain flour
1 egg, lightly beaten
250 g Clarified Butter (see page 175)
1 cup Roast Tomato Sauce (see page 178)
green salad, to serve

Rabbit liver faggots

100 g butter
2 medium brown onions, chopped
1 clove garlic, chopped
600 g rabbit meat, liver and kidneys,
    reserved from above
100 g fatty ham, diced
½ cup Toasted Herb Breadcrumbs
    (see page 175)
1 tablespoon chopped flat-leaf
    parsley leaves
3 sage leaves, chopped
½ teaspoon fennel seeds, ground
½ teaspoon coriander seeds, ground
salt, to taste
freshly ground black pepper, to taste
100 g caul fat (see page 172)

* Freeze the rabbit carcasses for stock
(follow the Chicken Stock recipe on
page 176) and the legs for another dish.

Faggots are tasty balls of coarsely minced pork and liver mixed with some breadcrumbs, onion and herbs, and wrapped in caul fat. They can be fried or baked.

Cut 2 fillets from each rabbit. Remove the livers and kidneys, then dice and reserve for the faggots. Cut enough meat from the front legs and belly flaps of the rabbits to make up 600 g when combined with the liver and kidneys, then dice and reserve for the faggots.

To make the faggots, preheat oven to 200°C. Melt butter in a saucepan and fry onions until brown. Add garlic, rabbit meat, liver and kidneys, and cook for a few minutes, until cooked through. Remove from heat and add ham, breadcrumbs, parsley, sage, ground fennel, ground coriander, salt and pepper. Roll mixture into 12 small balls then wrap each ball in caul fat, making sure not to overlap it too much, or it won't cook properly. Place on a baking tray and bake for about 15 minutes, until lightly browned.

Meanwhile, combine breadcrumbs, bacon and parsley. Dip rabbit fillets in flour, then egg and then breadcrumb mixture. Heat Clarified Butter in a frying pan and fry crumbed fillets for about 1 minute each side, until golden. They should be just cooked in the centre – do not overcook or they will be very dry. Leave to rest in a warm area for 5 minutes.

Heat Roast Tomato Sauce in a small saucepan. Pour 2 tablespoons sauce onto each plate and top with a sliced rabbit fillet and 2 faggots. Serve with a green salad.

Crumbed veal brains with veal hoof + ravigote sauce

Serves 6

1 veal hoof*
2 medium carrots, chopped
1 large brown onion, chopped
1 stick celery, chopped
4 cloves garlic, chopped
2 dried bay leaves
2 sprigs thyme
1 veal shank
pinch chopped garlic, extra
pinch grated lemon zest
pinch chopped thyme leaves, extra
salt, to taste
freshly ground black pepper, to taste
6 veal brains*
1 litre Vegetable Stock (see page 177)
½ cup plain flour
2 eggs, lightly beaten
1 cup Gremolata Breadcrumbs
    (see page 175)
3 turnips, peeled
250 g Clarified Butter (see page 175)
ravigote sauce, to serve (see page 51)

✱ Most butchers will be able to order veal hoof for you if you give them 1–2 weeks' notice. A good alternative, however, is veal tendons, which are readily available in Chinese butchers. Use 500 g tendons and cook for about the same time as the veal shank, until very tender. You can also substitute a pig's trotter (see page 38). You can use 12 lamb's brains (halved instead of quartered) instead of the 6 veal brains.

Arriving in Australia in 1970, I was surprised to discover that offal and 'extremities', so revered in European and Asian cooking for their flavour and texture, were discarded. How lucky for immigrants like me, who could buy all these cuts at a fraction of the price we would have paid in our home countries! Attitudes have changed with the years, and today dishes such as crumbed brains and grilled veal liver are as popular on restaurant menus as any other. These days you can also buy veal hoofs cleaned of hair . . . About 20 years ago, my eager-to-please butcher assured me he could get me veal hoofs, which he did, but didn't tell me they were coming with the hair still on! I tried to clean one myself, but, after an hour of perseverance, threw the lot in the bin. Ideally, start this dish the day before, as the veal hoof takes 6 hours to cook and the veal hoof roll should be refrigerated overnight.

The day before, bring a large saucepan of water to the boil. Add hoof and cook for 5 minutes (to blanch and remove impurities). Drain and return hoof to the pan with carrots, onion, celery, garlic, bay leaves and thyme. Cover with water and bring to the boil, reduce heat, cover and simmer for 3 hours, checking occasionally to make sure water hasn't evaporated too much. If it has, top up with a little boiling water.

Add the shank, top up water, and simmer for another hour or so, until the meat on the shank is tender and falls off the bone. Remove shank from pan, and continue to cook hoof for another 1–2 hours, until the meat falls off the bone. Meanwhile, remove all the meat from the shank, discard bone, cover meat and refrigerate.

When hoof is cooked, remove from heat and leave in cooking liquid until cool enough to handle. Place a 60 cm length of plastic film on a work surface and, while hoof is still warm, remove skin, in one piece if possible, and place it, skin-side down, on the plastic film. Sprinkle over extra garlic, lemon zest, extra thyme, salt and pepper. Cover with veal shank pieces and top with all the jellied meaty parts from the hoof, discarding the hoof bone. Using the plastic film as a guide, roll the skin up to form a thick sausage and wrap well in the plastic film, twisting the ends like a bonbon. Refrigerate overnight.

The next day, prepare the brains by soaking in cold water for 10 minutes. Change water and soak for another 10 minutes, then repeat this step once more to help loosen the surrounding membrane. Gently peel off the membrane – dipping the brains in fresh water as you work will help loosen it. Soak in fresh water for about another hour, until as much blood as possible is removed. Drain. Place brains in a saucepan with Vegetable Stock. Bring to the boil, reduce heat and simmer for 25 minutes. Drain brains and cover with plastic film, gently patting the film onto the surface. Refrigerate.

Remove plastic film from veal hoof sausage and slice sausage as thinly as possible. Leave to come to room temperature. Slice cold brains in half lengthwise, then cut each half on the diagonal into 2 slices. Dust with flour, dip in beaten egg and coat with Gremolata Breadcrumbs. Slice the turnips finely – a mandoline (see page 173) on the thickest setting is ideal for this.

Heat Clarified Butter in a frying pan and fry brains for a couple of minutes on each side until golden. Keep warm. Bring a pan of salted water to the boil and blanch turnips for 1 minute, until just cooked through. Drain well and arrange on 6 warmed plates. Place hoof sausage on top of the turnip slices and top with brains (the heat from the turnip slices and the brains will warm the hoof sausage just enough). Spoon over some ravigote sauce and put the rest on the table for your guests to help themselves.

Using leftovers

Don't waste the stock in which you cooked the hoof: freeze it and use it in soups or sauces. I've also served these poached veal brains as an entrée, cold, sliced and arranged on a bed of greens with ravigote sauce.

Stuffed pig's ears with green tartare sauce + watercress salad

Serves 8

8 pig's ears
2 medium carrots, roughly chopped
1 large brown onion, roughly chopped
½ stick celery, roughly chopped
6 cloves garlic, peeled
2 dried bay leaves
2 sprigs flat-leaf parsley
salt, to taste
freshly ground black pepper, to taste
½ cup white wine vinegar
250 g butter, melted
2 cups Fresh Breadcrumbs (see page 175)
green tartare sauce* (see page 4), to serve

Stuffing

500 g veal sweetbreads
1 cup Chicken Stock (see page 176)
125 g butter
2 large brown onions, chopped
500 g button mushrooms, diced
1 cup dry white wine
250 g ham, diced
1 tablespoon chopped thyme leaves
¼ cup chopped flat-leaf parsley leaves
salt, to taste
freshly ground black pepper, to taste

Watercress salad

2 bunches watercress, sprigs picked,
   washed and well dried
drizzle of red wine vinegar
drizzle of extra-virgin olive oil
salt, to taste
freshly ground black pepper, to taste

✱ If you don't want to make the green tartare sauce for this recipe, you can use Dijon mustard instead.

After arriving in Australia and becoming obsessed with cooking, I wanted to reassure myself that a career change from electrician to cook was possible. I was introduced to Stephanie Alexander by a friend who was working in her kitchen at the time and, as her second chef wanted to work a 4-day week, she gave me the opportunity to come in and help out on Saturdays. It was an amazing experience, trying to translate my domestic knowledge to a busy commercial kitchen where, instead of enjoying the gentle initiation of a young apprentice, who is given the most basic tasks, I was thrown in at the deep end, completing the second chef's unfinished job list, boning and stuffing quails and the like. One of my very first tasks was peeling the membranes off cooked sweetbreads and slicing them as thinly as possible for a salad. I've never forgotten it, as at the time it was one of the most exciting dishes I'd seen: turnips, sweetbreads, pistachios and thins strips of orange peel, with a walnut oil and orange vinaigrette.

Using a pair of tongs, hold pig's ears over an open flame to singe off any hairs. Don't leave them over the flame any longer than necessary; if the skin burns it will have an unpleasant taste. Wash thoroughly and put in a saucepan with carrots, onion, celery, garlic, bay leaves, parsley, salt, pepper, vinegar and enough water to cover. Bring to the boil, reduce heat and simmer for 2–3 hours, until a skewer goes easily through the ear cartilage. Leave in the cooking liquid until cool enough to handle.

Meanwhile, prepare stuffing by soaking the sweetbreads in plenty of salted water for 1 hour. Drain. Place sweetbreads in a saucepan with Chicken Stock, bring to the boil, reduce heat and simmer for 10 minutes. Remove sweetbreads from stock and squeeze gently to remove excess liquid. Return stock to the saucepan and set aside. When sweetbreads are cool enough to handle, gently peel off and discard the surrounding membrane and divide into small pieces.

Melt butter in a large frying pan and fry onions until golden. Add mushrooms and cook for a few minutes until they are soft and most of the liquid has evaporated. Add wine to the reserved stock, bring to the boil, then simmer until reduced to a quarter of its volume – it should look like a thick sauce. Remove from heat and stir in mushroom and onion mixture, sweetbreads, ham, thyme, parsley, salt and pepper. Allow to cool.

Remove an ear from the cooking liquid and trim base to form a neat triangle. Using a small knife and your fingers, carefully make a pocket in the ear between the skin and one side of the cartilage. Fill the pocket with one eighth of the stuffing. Wrap in plastic film and refrigerate cartilage-side down. Repeat with remaining ears and stuffing.➜

Preheat oven to 220°C. When ears are completely cold and set, remove from fridge. Brush both sides of ears with melted butter and cover well with breadcrumbs. Place ears on a non-stick baking tray, cartilage-side down, and bake for about 10 minutes, until golden brown.

Meanwhile, make watercress salad. Place watercress sprigs in a salad bowl, drizzle over vinegar and oil, sprinkle over salt and pepper, and toss well.

Place a cooked ear on each plate, cartilage-side up, with watercress salad beside it. Pass the green tartare sauce separately.

Some more ideas

Drain and freeze any leftover stock from cooking the pig's ears and use it in soups and sauces. The pig's ears can also be crumbed and baked without the stuffing, as is common in French bistros. Or you can stuff 12 small pig's ears (cut off the bottom of the ear to the desired size) as an entrée.

Serves 8

2.5 kg uncooked honeycomb green veal
     tripe, pre-washed by butcher
2 medium carrots, roughly chopped
1 large brown onion, roughly chopped
1 stick celery, roughly chopped
5 dried bay leaves
10 sprigs flat-leaf parsley
½ head garlic
250 g butter
2.5 kg brown onions, sliced
1 cup red wine vinegar
10 cloves garlic, chopped
3 teaspoons finely chopped thyme leaves
½ cup tomato paste
3 cups Veal Glaze (see page 176)
1½ tablespoons salt
1½ tablespoons freshly ground
     black pepper
½ cup finely chopped flat-leaf
     parsley leaves
green salad, to serve

When I arrived at Berowra Waters Inn in 1982, Gay Bilson wanted to keep only 3 dishes from the previous menu (and they remained on the menu until the restaurant closed in 1995). Tripes lyonnaises was one of them. I came to Berowra Waters after Tony Bilson had left, but his chef, Andrew Birley, was cooking the dish as he'd learnt it from Tony. The dish was assembled on the spot, using a handful of this, a touch of that and a dash of something else. The technician in me couldn't cope with the imprecision, and so I developed my own version, which is what we served thereafter and what you see here.

Place tripe, carrots, chopped onion, celery, bay leaves, parsley sprigs and ½ head garlic in a large non-aluminium pot, cover with cold water and bring to the boil, then reduce heat and simmer until tripe is soft. Depending on the tripe, this will take 3–7 hours. Allow tripe to cool in the water, then remove and refrigerate, discarding cooking water and vegetables.

Melt butter in a large non-stick frying pan with a lid and cook sliced onions, covered, over a low heat until they are very soft and seem to have 'melted'. Cut tripe into 5 mm wide strips and set aside. Uncover onions, increase heat and cook until they are dark brown but not burnt, stirring constantly and scraping the caramelised pieces off the bottom of the pan. Add vinegar, chopped garlic, thyme, tomato paste, Veal Glaze, salt and pepper, stir well and bring to the boil. Add tripe and mix well. Boil for 5 minutes or until tripe looks thick and glossy, stirring constantly to ensure tripe does not stick. Add chopped parsley and serve with the green salad.

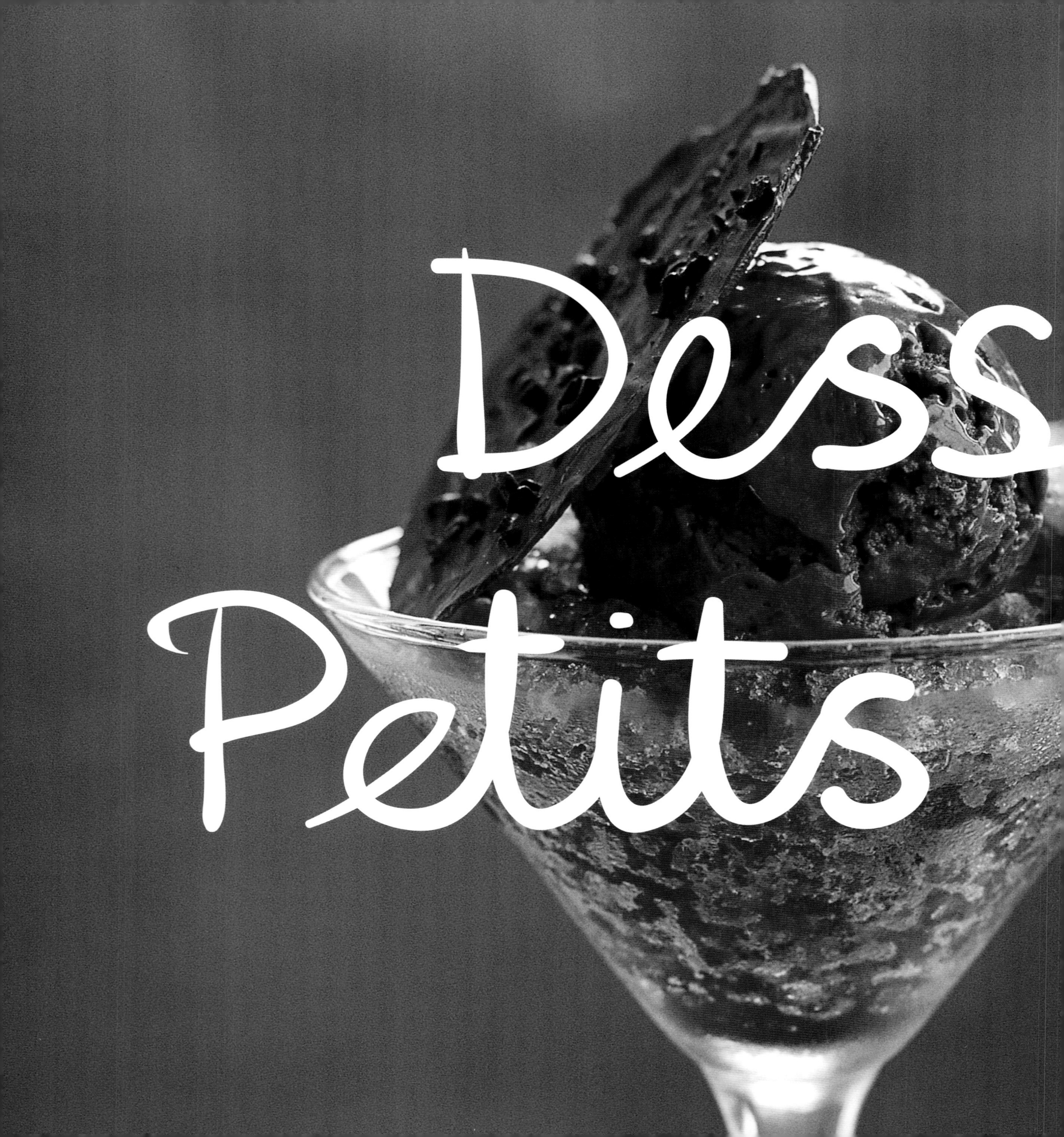
Dess
Petits

erts +
Fours

I never cooked for my father

'But I don't understand why you left such a brilliant career as an electrician to become a mere cook,' my father said.

My father was a wonderful man, a very intelligent man. He could speak perfect Turkish and he communicated well in French and German. He became a volunteer tutor, helping all the neighbourhood children with their studies simply because he loved helping and loved learning himself. Yet he remained a labourer all his life and he lived happily. His interest was helping his children, to the best of his ability, to achieve what they wanted to do with their lives. That's why I got a surprise when he came out with such a comment.

Growing up in Greece 50 years ago, if lack of finance prevented you from going to high school or university, you could go to technical college at night to learn a trade and work during the day. And if you were not clever enough for that, you could get a job in a restaurant, so at least you would not go hungry. This attitude has changed, of course, and today the career of a Greek chef is seen to be as important as any other.

Ten years after my arrival in Australia, David and I decided to visit Greece, for David to meet my parents, my brothers, George and Tassos, and their families. The meeting was nothing short of a disaster, and the only thing David remembers from that trip is the Greek salad we had on a hot day in an obscure little taverna in a small village, served icy cold on an aluminium plate. From where we were sitting we could see the tomatoes, cucumbers and capsicums growing in the garden among the olive trees and the goats. What a picture! In that environment anything would taste good. As for me, my brother George's company was enough to make me happy.

Father loved his food. He would question Mother if she said one of us needed a new pair of shoes, but he would never question the cost of food. He would always have a story to tell about food. Despite that, he never entered the kitchen and always expected Mother to pour him a glass of water at the table. Yet it was his job to bring water from outside to the kitchen in the water vessels. He loved Grandmother's garos as mezedes: salted, fermented entrails of fish, such as bonito or mackerel, kept in a sealed jar in a sunny spot for a month before being ready to eat spread on bread – a bit like fishy Vegemite, but not something I'd encourage anybody to try at home! 'It beats Russian caviar,' he would say. The recipe must go back 2000 years or more, as I have seen something similar in the Roman cookery of Apicius, a fish sauce called garum that was used extensively in Greek and Roman dishes of the day. Funny how we think we have just invented cuisine!

Other dishes I remember Father being fond of were stuffed spleen, and a pie made with rice, spring onions, dill, eggs and all the insides of the lamb, including the lungs, heart and throat. The final mixture was encased in caul fat to keep it moist and sent to the local baker's oven. It was not only the unusual dishes he liked. He liked everything about food. And the highlight, of course, was Grandma Domna's Karidato (see page 170).

One story of Father's that I always remember was about a dish he had in the Greek Navy while he was doing his national service. It consisted of layers of rice and a sauce of lamb's liver, onions, tomatoes and spices. The poor man must have been starving, to find a dish from a Greek Navy kitchen appetising! Mother never made the dish for him – she didn't know how.

Well, Dad, I often made that dish for you in my mind, planned how I could prepare it and serve it. But you aren't with us any longer to eat it . . .

Apple + raisin charlotte with calvados sauce

Serves 6

½ cup raisins*
½ cup calvados
6 Bramley or Granny Smith apples
150 g unsalted butter, softened
½ cup castor sugar
½ stick cinnamon
grated zest of 1 lemon
20 g butter, softened, extra
2 tablespoons castor sugar, extra
½ teaspoon ground cinnamon
1 loaf brioche, crusts removed,
    very thinly sliced
sweetened whipped cream, to serve

Calvados sauce*

500 g (approximately 6) Bramley
    or Granny Smith apples
1 cup apple juice (preferably made
    fresh at home)
grated zest and strained juice of 1 lemon
¼ vanilla bean
5 teaspoons calvados
2 tablespoons castor sugar
2½ tablespoons 35%-fat cream

✱ You can always use sultanas rather than raisins. If you wish, you can use the sherry sabayon sauce from page 149 instead of the calvados sauce. This dish can be prepared up until the baking step the day before, refrigerated, then baked straight from the fridge just before serving.

I was so happy a few years ago when Bramley apples became available in Australia for the first time. I knew of them from English cookbooks, and I think they're the best cooking apples available. They are now grown in Tasmania, and are in season from May to July; use them instead of the Granny Smiths if you can find them. This recipe works best if you soak the raisins in calvados overnight. The calvados sauce recipe makes about 500 ml – refrigerate any leftover and serve with any fruit tart or pie.

Start charlotte by soaking raisins in calvados for a few hours, or preferably overnight.

Make calvados sauce by peeling, coring and chopping apples. Place in a saucepan with apple juice, lemon zest and juice, and vanilla bean, then cook, covered, over a low heat until very soft. Remove vanilla bean and set aside. Place apple mixture in a blender with calvados and sugar, and blend to a purée. Scrape vanilla seeds into mixture, add cream, and blend to just combine. Keep warm.

To finish the charlotte, peel, core and thickly slice the apples. Combine 50 g of the unsalted butter with the ½ cup sugar in a small saucepan and heat until the sugar has dissolved and the mixture has just started to turn slightly brown, a butterscotch colour. Add apples and cinnamon stick, then reduce heat and cook for about 30 minutes, stirring occasionally, until apples are very soft but still are holding their shape. Remove and discard cinnamon stick. Crush some of the apple, leaving some chunks. Add the raisins and calvados and the lemon zest.

Preheat oven to 200°C. Use the 20 g extra butter to grease 6 × 200–250 ml dariole moulds generously (with a good layer of butter on the bottom so the charlottes don't stick). Sprinkle each mould with extra castor sugar and tap to remove excess. Sprinkle a pinch of the ground cinnamon around the inside of each mould.

Using a dariole mould as a guide, cut 6 discs from the brioche slices to fit the bottom of each mould and 6 discs to fit the top. Cut remaining slices into strips about 3 cm wide and long enough to fit the sides of the dariole moulds (about 7 slices per mould).

Melt the remaining unsalted butter and brush it over the brioche strips and discs. Place a small disc, buttered-side down, in the bottom of each mould and line the sides with about 5–7 strips, overlapping them slightly. Pile apple mixture into the moulds, almost to the top, then top with the larger disc of brioche, buttered-side up. Trim off any excess brioche that comes up over the edge of the dariole mould.✱ Bake for 10–12 minutes, until top is golden.

Place 2 tablespoons calvados sauce on each plate and unmould the charlottes onto the sauce. Serve with sweetened whipped cream.

Croustade of berries with citrus cream

Serves 6

2 tablespoons unsalted butter
2 small candied clementines (see page 172),
    cut into thin segments (see page 174)
¼ piece cedro,* shaved
3 cups mixed berries (including some
    hulled and sliced strawberries)
1 tablespoon castor sugar
2 tablespoons Grand Marnier

Citrus cream

4 egg yolks
¼ cup castor sugar
½ cup strained orange juice
½ cup strained pink grapefruit juice
2 teaspoons strained lemon juice
1½ tablespoons Grand Marnier

Pastis pastry

1 egg, separated
small pinch salt
2 teaspoons olive oil
100 ml tepid water
250 g plain flour
plain flour, extra, for rolling dough
40 g unsalted butter, melted
¼ teaspoon ground cinnamon
3 teaspoons white sugar

✽ Cedro is a yellow–green candied citrus
fruit available at delicatessens and specialist
food shops. Cut cedro into shavings using
a potato peeler. The rather unusual beating
of this dough helps to develop elasticity, so
it can be stretched thinly without breaking.
Roll it with a rolling pin and stretch it by
hand if you don't have a pasta machine,
but it needs to be as thin as filo or strudel
dough. The croustade shells can be shaped
and left at room temperature for a couple
of hours until needed.

Pastis pastry resembles sheets of homemade filo pastry, and is traditionally used for croustades. At MG Garage, pastry chef Katrina MacDonald found my pasta machine useful for the first stage of the croustade. After the final roll, she stretched the dough by hand as thinly as possible. The dough is enough for 20 croustade shells; freeze leftover pastry and use instead of filo.

To make the citrus cream, whisk egg yolks with half the sugar until pale. Combine fruit juices and remaining sugar in a small saucepan and heat until almost boiling. Slowly pour hot juice into egg mixture, whisking constantly. Return mixture to saucepan and stir constantly with a wooden spoon over a *low* heat until the custard thickens enough to coat the back of the spoon. Strain into a bowl sitting in ice, add Grand Marnier and stir until cool. Refrigerate until required.

Make pastis dough by beating egg white with salt until stiff. Combine egg yolk and oil and fold into beaten egg white. Gradually add water while mixing, then continue mixing until smooth. Sift flour onto bench and make a well in the centre. Pour egg mixture into the well and, with a fork, start to incorporate the flour into the liquid. Mix with your fingers until all the flour is incorporated, then knead to form a smooth dough. Knead into a ball and beat with a rolling pin for 5 minutes, folding 20–30 times until springy and smooth.✽ Roll into a ball, cover with plastic film and leave at room temperature for 4–6 hours.

Unwrap dough and cut off one-third (freeze the rest). Roll the dough through a pasta machine, using plenty of extra flour to avoid sticking. Keep rolling until you reach the thinnest setting on the machine, then roll at least 3 times until pastry is paper-thin. If it gets too long to handle, cut it into manageable pieces. Stretch each piece gently with your hands in all directions until it is about 25 cm wide (thin enough to read a newspaper through). Allow dough to dry on a clean cloth for 10 minutes to an hour, depending on the humidity, until it is just flexible but not so dry that it will break.

Preheat oven to 200°C. Cut pastry into 6 × 25 cm discs. Brush with melted butter, and sprinkle with cinnamon and sugar. Gently take each disc and, with your thumbs in the centre, loosely crumple the edges in, to create a shell for the fruit filling – the base should be about 10 cm in diameter and the loose sides about 3 cm high.✽ If the sides of the shell start collapsing, the pastry is too wet and needs to dry a bit longer. The idea is to make a shell with as much surface area as possible, so there'll be lots of crunchy pastry when it's cooked. Bake on a baking tray for 3–5 minutes, until crisp and golden.

Meanwhile, heat butter in a frying pan until it just foams, then add clementines, cedro, berries and sugar, toss to just warm through, add Grand Marnier and remove from heat.

Top each pastry shell with berries and serve immediately. Pass citrus cream separately.

Deep-fried figs with walnut + pomegranate

Serves 6
vegetable oil, for deep-frying
1 cup plain flour
½ teaspoon baking powder
1 cup cold sparkling mineral water
    or soda water
18 small ripe figs
3 tablespoons chopped walnuts
seeds of 1 pomegranate
Basic Vanilla Parfait, to serve (see page 139)

Pomegranate sauce
1 tablespoon castor sugar
1 tablespoon boiling water
2 tablespoons pomegranate molasses*
2 tablespoons grenadine

* Pomegranate molasses is available in Middle-Eastern delicatessens.

Once, towards the end of fig season, when this dish was taken off the MG Garage menu, we suddenly discovered 2 trays of figs left in the cool room. My second chef, Lauren Murdoch, put them in a pan with sugar syrup, a couple of sticks of cinnamon and some lemon zest, and cooked them very gently for a couple of hours, until they were sitting in a thick, rich syrup. We used them in a tart similar to the Pink Grapefruit Peel & Almond Tart (see page 154). They reminded me so much of the preserved figs of my childhood that I took a large jar home and they lasted in the refrigerator for 3 years: I rationed myself 1 fig a month as a spoon sweet. I find it fascinating that the honey-like syrup preserved the figs so well.

To make the pomegranate sauce, dissolve castor sugar in boiling water then mix with pomegranate molasses and grenadine. Set aside to cool to room temperature.

Heat oil for deep-frying. Make batter by combining flour and baking powder in a mixing bowl then gently stirring in enough sparkling water to make a thin batter. I test it by dipping a fork into the batter: when lifted out it should cling between the tines for just a second before running off. Do not over-mix, and *do* use immediately, before it gets warm.

Dip figs into batter and drop into hot oil. Don't cook too many at a time, or the oil temperature will drop. Cook for a couple of minutes until golden, then drain well on kitchen paper.

Place 3 figs on each plate and spoon over a little pomegranate sauce. Sprinkle over chopped walnuts and pomegranate seeds and serve with Basic Vanilla Parfait.

Quince blancmange with poached quinces

Serves 6
600 g quince
1 litre water
muslin
1 cup 35%-fat cream
2½ leaves gelatine (see page 172)
50 g white sugar

Dark poached quinces
4 cups water
4 cups white sugar
2 star anise
3 cloves
1 cinnamon stick
10 black peppercorns
3 quinces

Light poached quinces
4 cups water
4 cups white sugar
40 g ginger, peeled and sliced
3 quinces

✽ If you like quinces but this blancmange seems too complicated, cut quinces in half, scoop out the core, put 1 tablespoon honey in the cavity, then bake at 175°C for a couple of hours and serve with thick cream.

Greeks love quinces. As a child I used to eat them raw, just to see the adults pull a sour face. I still eat them raw when I find a very ripe one – not for the effect any longer, but just because I enjoy the flavour. I have used quinces in various recipes, including savoury dishes and a quince purée; roasted quarters of quince cooked in butter go very well with pork. It's best to start this dessert the day before you want to serve it.

The day before, start the blancmange by cutting unpeeled quinces into large chunks. Place in a saucepan, seeds and all, with water. Cover with a tight-fitting lid and simmer to a pulp, for about 2 hours, depending on how ripe the quinces are. Hang quince pulp in muslin over a bowl overnight to collect the liquid.

To make the dark poached quinces, preheat oven to 90°C. Combine water, sugar and spices in an ovenproof dish and bring to the boil, then remove from heat. Peel and quarter quinces (I leave the cores in while they're cooking, to help hold the quarters together). Add quinces and peelings to the dish and bring to a simmer. Cover and place in the oven for about 8 hours, until quinces are soft and dark brown (including the peelings helps make the quinces as dark as possible). Cool then refrigerate in syrup.

To make the light poached quinces, combine water, sugar and ginger in a saucepan and bring to the boil, then remove from heat. Peel and quarter the quinces one at a time, adding them to the sugar syrup as soon as they're prepared, to prevent them discolouring. Return saucepan to the heat and bring syrup to the boil. Reduce heat to a simmer and poach quinces until soft, about 30–40 minutes depending on their ripeness. Cool then refrigerate overnight in syrup, so they absorb as much ginger flavour as possible.

The next day, finish the blancmange by whipping the cream and refrigerating until required. Soak gelatine in cold water for 5 minutes. Remove quince pulp from muslin and discard. Combine 1 cup quince liquid with sugar in a small saucepan and heat until sugar is dissolved. Squeeze gelatine very well to remove as much water as possible. Add to the quince liquid and stir over a low heat until thoroughly dissolved. Strain into a bowl sitting in ice and stir until mixture just starts to thicken. Immediately fold cream in thoroughly and pour into 6 rinsed coffee cups or ½ cup moulds and refrigerate for a few hours until set.

Place 1 cup light poaching liquid (retaining the remainder) in a small saucepan and boil until reduced by about half. Set aside to cool. If it becomes too thick when cold, add a little more of the retained poaching liquid to bring it to the desired consistency. Remove quince pieces from their poaching liquids and cut out cores. Place 1 tablespoon dark poaching liquid in the centre of each plate. Arrange 2 light and 2 dark quarters on top and lightly glaze them with the reduced poaching liquid. Unmould a blancmange on the side.

mandarin jelly with spiced orange salad

Serves 6
1 packed tablespoon finely grated
     mandarin* zest
1 cup hot Sugar Syrup (see page 179)
2 cups strained mandarin* juice
4½ leaves gelatine (see page 172)

Spiced orange salad
6–8 large oranges*
1 packed teaspoon finely grated mandarin*
     zest
3 tablespoons Sugar Syrup (see page 179)
3 tablespoons strained mandarin* juice
3 small candied clementines* (see page
     172), cut into thin wedges
3 tablespoons diced cedro*
6 dates, stoned and cut into matchsticks
     then rolled in castor sugar
6 mint leaves, thinly sliced
18 pistachio nuts, shelled and thinly sliced
sprinkling Ras El Hanout (see page 177)

✱ If mandarins aren't available, use any
other citrus fruit. Tangelos or blood
oranges can be substituted for the oranges
in the salad (allow 12, as both are smaller).
Any other candied citrus can be used
instead of the candied clementines. Cedro
is a yellow–green candied citrus fruit
available at delicatessens and specialty
food shops.

It's great to use fresh pistachios in this salad. When they're in season,
I love to serve a bowl of pistachios with drinks; the contrast of the pink
outer skin with the green kernel is so beautiful.

To make the jelly, mix mandarin zest into hot (not boiling) Sugar Syrup and leave to steep
for 5 minutes. Stir in the mandarin juice. Soak gelatine in 1 cup of the Sugar Syrup and
mandarin liquid for 5 minutes. Heat through over a very low heat to dissolve gelatine
then mix into the rest of the liquid. Rinse and drain 6 × ½ cup moulds (tea cups or dariole
moulds are suitable) – this makes it easier to unmould the jellies. Strain jelly into moulds
and refrigerate until set.

   To make the spiced orange salad, peel the oranges and cut into segments (see page
174), retaining the juice. Put segments into a bowl then squeeze the remaining pulp over
the bowl to extract the juice. Combine mandarin zest and Sugar Syrup in a small saucepan. Bring to the boil, remove from heat and set aside to cool. Stir in mandarin juice and
pour over the orange segments. Set aside to marinate for at least 1 hour.

   Unmould each jelly onto the centre of a plate and surround with the orange segments
and some of the juice. Arrange clementines, cedro, sugar-coated dates, mint leaves and
pistachio nuts around each plate and sprinkle with Ras El Hanout.

Chocolate mousse + coffee granita

Serves 10

300 g semi-sweet (57%-cocoa) couverture
    chocolate (see page 172)
2 eggs
5 egg yolks
¾ cup white sugar
¼ cup water
1½ cups 35%-fat cream
½ cup castor sugar
1 litre weak black espresso or
    plunger coffee
250 g semi-sweet (57%) couverture
    chocolate, extra
1 tablespoon coffee beans, coarsely
    ground
300 ml 35%-fat cream, extra, whipped,
    to serve

✱ This chocolate mousse can also be
served by itself with 1 tablespoon cream
and a biscuit. For a coffee granita with
a twist, try making it with Greek coffee
flavoured with cardamom.

This rich, French-influenced chocolate mousse is served with a refreshing
Italian-style coffee granita. I like the contrast of the 2 dishes in this dessert.
It could never be taken off the menu at MG Garage, as it was my friend
Roberta's favourite.

Cut the 300 g chocolate into pieces, place in a bowl over a saucepan of hot (definitely
not boiling) water (making sure the bowl does not touch the water), allow to melt completely, then keep lukewarm (if the chocolate cools down too much it will be hard to
incorporate and might leave lumps). Whisk eggs and egg yolks in the bowl of an electric
mixer until pale – almost white – and full of air. Meanwhile, combine the ¾ cup sugar
and water in a small saucepan, heat gently until all the sugar dissolves, then boil until a
drop of the syrup forms a soft ball when dropped into cold water. *Slowly* add sugar syrup
to the eggs – drizzle it down the side of the bowl rather than pouring it straight into the
middle, and whisk the whole time. Continue whisking until egg mixture is cool. Fold in
melted chocolate; avoid over-folding, as it will deflate the egg mixture. Whisk cream to
soft peaks (do not over-whisk or it will be hard to incorporate) and fold into the chocolate
mixture. Refrigerate until set.

    To make the granita, add extra castor sugar to the coffee, to your taste – you may not
need all of it but it should be sweet, since you're using it in a dessert. Pour liquid into a
shallow metal tray and place in the freezer. When it has just started to freeze (it will take
a few hours to freeze completely, depending on the freezer), scrape with a fork to create
granita flakes and return to freezer. Repeat scraping a few more times during freezing
and again just before serving.

    Meanwhile, melt the extra chocolate (using the same method as above) and spread
into 10 very, very thin discs on baking paper or plastic film. Sprinkle with ground coffee
beans and refrigerate to set. Cut disks into a neat circle using a round cutter or knife and
keep in the refrigerator until the moment they are to be used.

    To serve, place coffee granita in the bottom of a martini glass. Make a hole in the
middle and top with 1 tablespoon extra whipped cream, then 1 nicely shaped tablespoon
chocolate mousse. Place a chocolate disc on top and serve immediately.

Double-baked chocolate soufflés with baked strawberries + chocolate sauce

Serves 6

225 ml egg whites (from about 7 eggs)
pinch cream of tartar*
180 g castor sugar
60 g cocoa powder*
1 teaspoon ground cinnamon
castor sugar, extra, to sprinkle in cups
1–2 cups 35%-fat cream (depending
    on size of baking dish)
Strawberry Ice-cream (see page 138),
    to serve (optional)

Chocolate sauce

100 ml weak black coffee
100 g icing sugar
50 g cocoa powder*
100 ml 35%-fat cream
100 g semi-sweet (57%) couverture
    chocolate (see page 172), chopped
1 tablespoon brandy

Baked strawberries

30 medium strawberries*
1 cup castor sugar

✱ If whisking egg whites for meringues or
soufflés is part of your cooking repertoire,
it's worth investing in a copper bowl,
which makes the task quicker and delivers
lighter results. If you have a copper bowl,
omit the cream of tartar from the recipe.
Always buy pure cocoa powder of the best
quality. Use more or fewer strawberries,
depending on their size.

Many people are unnecessarily afraid of making soufflés. Double-baked soufflés are a fail-proof method – the initial baking can be done a few hours ahead of time, then the soufflés can be turned out, covered in cream and baked just before they are to be served. If you still have concerns about soufflé-making, just call them 'puddings' instead of 'soufflés', as I did when I had to serve 500 of them at a charity dinner (which was just as well, as a 20-minute speech began just as we were about to serve them).

Preheat oven to 125°C. Whisk egg whites with cream of tartar, until soft peaks form. Slowly add a third of the sugar, whisking all the time, and continue until stiff peaks form. Sift over the remaining sugar, with the cocoa and cinnamon, and fold in very lightly, so as not to deflate the egg whites.

Grease 6 × 200 ml cups or moulds with butter, sprinkle with castor sugar and tap to remove excess. Divide soufflé mixture among the cups. Bake in a bain-marie (see page 174) half-filled with hot water for 20 minutes. Turn oven off and leave soufflés in bain-marie in oven for another 20 minutes. Remove bain-marie from oven, cover loosely with foil, and set aside until needed.

To make the chocolate sauce, pour coffee into a small saucepan. Sift over icing sugar and cocoa and whisk into the coffee. Bring to the boil, whisking all the time. Add cream, chocolate and brandy and stir over a low heat until chocolate has melted.

Preheat oven to 220°C. To make the baked strawberries, hull the strawberries then wash and drain them well. Toss strawberries in castor sugar just to coat, then arrange in a baking dish in a single layer, spreading them out as much possible.

Turn soufflés out into a small baking dish that will allow them enough room to expand. Gently pour over cream until it fills the dish to a depth of 1 cm.

Place soufflés and strawberries in the oven. Bake soufflés for 5–10 minutes, until they have puffed up again, and strawberries until sugar starts to caramelise. The strawberries should retain their shape – don't cook them beyond this point, or they'll become mushy.

Lift each soufflé carefully onto a serving plate and place 5 strawberries on each plate with some of the juices from the baking dish. Pour over chocolate sauce and serve Strawberry Ice-cream on the side if desired.

Gold-leaf chocolate pyramid

Serves 40

First chocolate génoise
6 × 60 g eggs
1 cup castor sugar
110 g plain flour
40 g cocoa powder*
100 g Clarified Butter (see page 175),
    melted

Flourless chocolate cake
900 g semi-sweet (57%) couverture
    chocolate (see page 172)
½ cup brandy
160 ml weak espresso coffee (long black)
    or 3 tablespoons instant coffee in
    160 ml hot water
12 × 60 g eggs
1 cup castor sugar
2 cups 35%-fat cream

Second chocolate génoise
6 × 60 g eggs
1 cup castor sugar
110 g plain flour
40 g cocoa powder
100 g Clarified Butter (see page 175),
    melted

First chocolate ganache
250 g semi-sweet (57%) couverture
    chocolate
180 ml 35%-fat cream

Second chocolate ganache
250 g semi-sweet (57%) couverture
    chocolate
180 ml 35%-fat cream

To assemble
½ cup brandy
½ cup Sugar Syrup (see page 179)
250 g semi-sweet (57%) couverture
    chocolate
50 leaves pure 23-carat loose gold leaf*

Years ago, Stephanie Alexander told me she wanted to make the richest chocolate cake imaginable, and I suggested, as a joke, that we stick gold leaf on it. My joke fell on deaf ears at the time, but the idea stayed in my mind until we wanted to do something special for Phillip Searle's 40th birthday at Berowra Waters Inn. When I opened MG Garage, I decided to use the cake as a signature dish, to say to my customers, with tongue in cheek, 'This is the richest food I can give you.' The first gold-leaf chocolate pyramid I made was a metre high – it was for the wedding of my friends Anita and Garnet. It was very exciting, creating such a cake, which had to be hollow in the centre, with layers of cake to create the pyramid walls. I proudly delivered the cake to the wedding reception and, on arrival, realised my BIG mistake: I had made an Egyptian pyramid for a Jewish wedding! Not thinking about the religious or political implications, I had made a pyramid to signify durability and stability. My gesture wasn't enough, however, as 10 years later the couple separated . . . but their wedding guests are still asking about the significance of the cake.

For this recipe you'll need: 1 × 22 cm square, deep cake tin; 1 × 15 cm square, deep cake tin; and 2 × 38 cm × 25 cm Swiss roll tins. If you can't find tins with these exact dimensions, you can compromise and adjust the assembly accordingly. All the baking tins need to be prepared by buttering them, lining them with baking paper, buttering the paper, dusting it with flour, then inverting and tapping the tins to remove excess flour. If you don't have enough wire racks to cool the cakes, they can be cooled on clean tea towels.

To make the first chocolate génoise, preheat oven to 175°C, then whisk eggs and sugar over a bowl of hot (not boiling) water until lukewarm and sugar has dissolved. Remove bowl from water and continue whisking until mixture has cooled and forms a ribbon-like pattern on top of the mixture for a few seconds when you lift out the whisk.

Gradually sift combined flour and cocoa over the egg mixture and fold in gradually. Once you have added three-quarters of the flour, fold in the Clarified Butter and the remaining flour alternately. Divide mixture between 2 greased and lined, deep cake tins: 1 × 22 cm square and 1 × 15 cm square. Ensure mixture comes to an equal height in both tins. Bake for 30 minutes, then test with a thin metal skewer – it should come out clean once the cakes are cooked. The small cake should be cooked first, and the large cake should take a further 10 minutes to finish cooking. Leave each cake in its tin to rest for 5 minutes before turning it out onto a wire rack to cool.→

Next make the flourless chocolate cake. Reduce oven temperature to 150°C. Combine chocolate, brandy and coffee in a bowl then sit bowl over a saucepan of hot (not boiling) water until chocolate has melted. Keep lukewarm. Using an electric mixer, whisk together eggs and castor sugar, until mixture falling from the beaters forms a ribbon-like pattern on top of the mixture for a few seconds. Whisk cream until soft peaks form. Fold a quarter of the egg mixture into the chocolate mixture until well combined. Gently fold through remaining egg mixture until just combined (do not over-mix; the chocolate will deflate the eggs). Fold in whipped cream. Divide mixture between 2 greased and lined, deep cake tins: 1 × 22 cm square and 1 × 15 cm square. Ensure mixture comes to an equal height in both tins. Seal both tins with baking paper then foil, securing well. Place each tin in a baking dish just large enough to hold it, then pour in enough boiling water to fill the dish to a depth of 5 cm. Bake for 1 hour.

After 1 hour, remove cakes from oven and test with a thin metal skewer – it should come out with some cooked mixture clinging to it. If the mixture clinging to the skewer still looks frothy, the cake needs to be returned to the oven for a further 15 minutes, then tested again. The large cake should take a further 15 minutes once the small cake is cooked. Remove cooked cakes from oven and leave to cool in their water baths. When cool, remove tins from water then remove foil and baking paper. Leave cakes in tins.

Make up the second chocolate génoise mixture following the same recipe as for the first. Increase oven temperature to 175°C. Divide mixture evenly between 2 greased and lined 38 × 25 cm Swiss roll tins. Bake for 15 minutes, then test with a thin metal skewer, which should come out clean once cakes are cooked. Leave cakes to rest in the tins for 2 minutes before turning out onto a wire rack to cool.

Make the first chocolate ganache once all cakes have cooled completely. Melt chocolate in a bowl over a saucepan of hot water then set aside until lukewarm. Whip cream to soft peaks then fold into lukewarm chocolate.

To assemble the cake, cut the 2 first génoises in half horizontally and open out, cut-side up. Combine ¼ cup of the brandy with ¼ cup of the Sugar Syrup and sprinkle over génoises, then spread all 4 cut sides with the first ganache. Place one half of the small génoise on top of the small flourless cake (still inside its tin), ganache-side down. Place 2 long sheets of plastic film on the work surface (they need to be long enough to wrap the cake in) and tip the cake tin upside-down onto the plastic film. Carefully remove the cake tin, leaving the cake sitting on the plastic film. Wash and dry cake tin. With the help of the plastic film, lift the cake and lower plastic film and cake into the clean tin. Place the other half of the small génoise on top of the cake, ganache-side down. Wrap the plastic film over the top of the cake and refrigerate for a few hours or overnight.

Repeat with large génoise halves and large flourless cake.

When cakes are cold and have set, cut a thick piece of cardboard into a 24 cm square as a base for the cake. Cover the cardboard in plastic film. Unwrap the top of the large cake. Place the cardboard square over the cake tin, ensuring that the tin is centred, then tip the cake upside-down onto the cardboard on a work surface and carefully remove the tin and plastic film. Unwrap the top of the small cake and tip it upside-down onto the centre of the large cake then carefully remove the tin and plastic film.

At this stage you should have the start of an Inca-style pyramid (with one step). You'll need to use your imagination to construct the rest of the pyramid. Using a large knife dipped in boiling water, carefully cut the large cake diagonally from the outer edge of the small cake to the outer edge of the large cake on all 4 sides, reserving the off-cuts.

Repeat this process with the small cake, starting about 2 cm from the edge and cutting diagonally to the outer edge. Make sure the knife is constantly hot as you cut, otherwise the cake won't cut easily and will crumble.

Cut the largest of the off-cuts in half and place on top of the small cake to form the third layer of the pyramid. Trim the sides of this third layer diagonally to form the correct shape. Don't worry if the shape isn't perfect at this stage, as the final layer of cake will cover any imperfections.

Make the second ganache using the same method as for the first.

Lean one of the rectangular second génoise cakes against one side of the pyramid so that the bottom left-hand corner of the cake is flush with the bottom left edge of the pyramid. Using the pyramid as a guide, trim the left side to the shape of the pyramid. Trim the right side to the pyramid shape, leaving a 1 cm margin. Turn the larger of the 2 off-cuts upside down and lean it against the next side of the pyramid, nestling it into the 1 cm overhang from the first piece. Trim the right side to the shape of the pyramid, again allowing a 1 cm margin. Repeat with the other rectangular second génoise, to cover the remaining 2 sides of the pyramid.

Spread one side of each of the 4 newly cut triangles of génoise with second ganache and stick them to the sides of the pyramid. Use remaining ganache to fill any gaps and to smooth joins. Combine the remaining ¼ cup brandy and ¼ cup Sugar Syrup and, using a pastry brush, sprinkle over the cake. Melt chocolate in a bowl over a saucepan of hot (not boiling) water. Lay a large piece of plastic film on the work surface and spread chocolate into a 1 mm thick triangle the same size as the sides of the pyramid. (It's easier to spread out the chocolate smoothly if the plastic film sticks to the work surface; this happens when the work surface is slightly damp.)

Carefully lift up plastic film and press chocolate onto one side of the pyramid. Gently smooth with your hands, leaving the plastic film in place. Repeat with the opposite →

✳ Always buy pure cocoa powder of the best quality. The gold leaf must be pure 23-carat in order to be edible – any lower grade means that it is mixed with another metal and can't be eaten. It should also be loose gold leaf rather than gold leaf with a backing, as the backing can be difficult to remove. You can buy gold leaf from art suppliers, but bear in mind that there is a lot of wastage. If you're planning on making this pyramid cake for a special occasion, I strongly recommend you practise on a smaller scale first, to perfect the assembly and also the gold leaf application. This cake freezes well for up to 2 months – wrap it tightly in baking paper and then in foil, place in an airtight freezer bag and freeze.

side of the pyramid and refrigerate until chocolate is set. Carefully peel plastic film back just from the edge of each triangle, folding it over so that it doesn't get caught under the chocolate coating of the adjoining side. Repeat process to coat remaining sides in chocolate and refrigerate until set.

A couple of hours before serving, remove cake from refrigerator and carefully peel off plastic film. Using a sheet of tissue paper to manipulate the gold leaves as required, gently press the gold leaves onto the chocolate. It's important that this be done in a draught-free place, as the gold leaf is so light that it can easily blow away. Serve at room temperature. It looks spectacular on a silver platter surrounded with pomegranate seeds or any berries.

An easier gold-leaf chocolate cake

Of course, you don't have to make a pyramid-shaped cake, although, if you do attempt the pyramid, children will always be eager to help! At MG Garage we used to make brick-shaped cakes in bread tins and serve thin slices with coffee. And if this elaborate recipe is too daunting, you can simply make your favourite chocolate cake, coat it in melted chocolate and finish it with pure 23-carat gold leaf.

Coffee cardamom + hazelnut custards

Serves 12

Coffee cardamom custard
600 ml 35%-fat cream
4 tablespoons coffee beans, crushed
½ teaspoon cardamom seeds, ground
6 egg yolks
2 eggs
½ cup castor sugar

Hazelnut custard
1 tablespoon hazelnut paste*
600 ml 35%-fat cream
6 egg yolks
2 eggs
½ cup castor sugar

Coffee jelly
2 leaves gelatine (see page 172)
1 cup very weak black coffee
2 tablespoons castor sugar

Caramel jelly
2 leaves gelatine
⅔ cup castor sugar
1⅓ cup water
1 tablespoon Frangelico* (optional)

✻ Hazelnut paste is available in health food shops. You will need only a small amount of each of the jellies to glaze the custards; set the remainder and serve with another dessert. Frangelico is an Italian hazelnut liqueur.

I once had Turkish coffee granita with cardamom on the menu, and a customer asked me, 'Why Turkish coffee when you're Greek?' 'Because,' I replied, 'I'm a cook looking for flavours, not politics, and I associate cardamom with Middle-Eastern and Turkish flavours rather than Greek ones.'

To make the coffee custard, mix cream, coffee beans and ground cardamom in a small saucepan and heat until just boiling. Remove from heat, cover and set aside in a warm place to infuse for about 30 minutes. Stir together egg yolks, eggs and sugar until well combined. Strain hot cream into the egg mixture stirring constantly until well combined. Pour into 12 × ¼ cup custard pots (or espresso cups) and remove any bubbles from the top using either a spoon or plastic film. Cover each pot with foil. Preheat oven to 150°C.

To make the hazelnut custard, dissolve hazelnut paste in a little of the cream. Pour remaining cream into a small saucepan, heat until just boiling, then remove from heat. Stir together egg yolks, eggs, sugar and remaining hazelnut paste until well combined. Strain hot cream into egg mixture, and stir until well combined. Pour into 12 × ¼ cup custard pots (or espresso cups) and remove any bubbles. Cover each pot with foil.

Bake all custards in a bain-marie (see page 174) with the water halfway up the sides of the custard pots for about 20 minutes, until firm to the touch. Remove from oven, allow to cool, then refrigerate custards until well chilled.

To make the coffee jelly, soak the gelatine in a little cold water for 2–3 minutes to soften then squeeze gently to remove as much water as possible. Combine coffee, sugar and gelatine in a small saucepan over a low heat until gelatine is completely dissolved. Leave to cool to room temperature and, when cool but not yet set, pour a little* over the top of each coffee custard, forming a thin layer to give a mirror-like finish. It's important that the mixture be no longer hot, or the finish will look cloudy.

To make the caramel jelly, soak the gelatine in a little cold water for 2–3 minutes to soften. Dissolve sugar in ⅓ cup of the water in a small saucepan and cook over a high heat until it turns a pale caramel colour. Remove from heat and leave for a minute or so, then carefully stir in remaining water. Return to heat and stir for a minute to ensure all the caramel has dissolved into the water. Squeeze gelatine gently to remove as much water as possible, add to the saucepan and stir over a low heat until gelatine is completely dissolved. Remove from heat and stir in Frangelico, if using. Leave to cool to room temperature, and when cool but not yet set, pour a little over the top of each hazelnut custard, forming a thin layer to give a mirror-like finish.

Place the 2 pots side by side on a serving plate. Serve with biscuits if you like, such as Florentines (see page 166).

Beaumes de Venise custard with poached cape gooseberries

Serves 6
1 cup 35%-fat cream
½ cup Beaumes de Venise*
1 small egg
4 large egg yolks
80 g castor sugar

Poached cape gooseberries
3 cups Sugar Syrup (see page 179)
½ cup water
grated zest and strained juice of ½ lemon
500 g cape gooseberries, husk removed

* This custard can be made with any dessert wine – I have used Sauternes, Muscat of Alexandria, Muscat de Rivesaltes and, of course, the Greek dessert wine Samos. The custard should be stirred gently, not beaten or whisked, to avoid forming bubbles that would ruin its texture.

I first made this custard using Samos wine, a dessert wine from the small Greek island of the same name, which is similar to Beaumes de Venise in taste. We loved the flavour in the restaurant but hardly any customers ordered the dish because they were unfamiliar with the wine. I changed the wine to Beaumes de Venise and *voilà* – bestseller!

To poach the gooseberries, combine Sugar Syrup, water, lemon zest and juice in a medium saucepan and bring to the boil. Add cape gooseberries, reduce heat to low and simmer for a few minutes until gooseberries are just soft. Allow to cool to room temperature.

Meanwhile, make the custard by preheating oven to 150°C. Heat cream and Beaumes de Venise separately to just below their boiling points. Stir* egg, egg yolks and sugar until very well combined. Slowly pour hot Beaumes de Venise into to egg mixture, stirring constantly, then add hot cream, stirring constantly. Strain and discard any foam. Pour into 6 greased ½ cup dariole moulds, remove any bubbles from the top of the custard using a teaspoon or plastic film, then cover each mould with foil and bake in a bain-marie (see page 174) for 15–20 minutes, until a thin metal skewer comes out clean. Refrigerate until cold.

Unmould custards onto serving plates and serve the cape gooseberries on the side with some of their poaching syrup.

'Squeeze, freeze, scratch and serve' is almost the only recipe you need for granitas. They are one of my favourite desserts, for their simplicity and the refreshment they provide at the end of a meal. They are so easy, can be flavoured with whatever you like, and look great served in a martini glass. I have not given a number of portions for these recipes, but think of about ⅔ cup unfrozen liquid per serve. Any leftover granitas can be kept in the freezer and are always welcome. We served many other granitas at MG Garage. Janine Nicholson, our 'Beverage Engineer' (as we affectionately called her) made a delicious pomegranate sangria that we also froze into a granita.

Lavender granita
½ bunch fresh French lavender* (yielding
    ½ packed cup flowers)
1 litre water
250 g castor sugar
100 ml strained lemon juice

✱ Do not use thin-stemmed English lavender for this recipe, as the flowers are more bitter than those of the thicker-stemmed French lavender.

Combine flowers with half the water and bring to the boil. Set aside until lukewarm. Strain, reserving liquid and squeezing flowers well to remove as much liquid as possible. Add sugar to strained liquid and stir well to dissolve, then add remaining water and lemon juice. Pour into a shallow metal tray and place in the freezer. When it has just started to freeze (it will take a few hours to freeze completely, depending on the freezer), scrape with a fork to create granita flakes and return to freezer. Repeat scraping a few more times during freezing and again just before serving.

Watermelon, honeydew melon & rockmelon granitas
½ watermelon
1 honeydew melon
1 knob preserved ginger
1 rockmelon
kirsch, to taste
castor sugar, to taste (optional)

Scoop flesh out of watermelon and squeeze through a fine sieve. Scoop flesh out of honeydew melon and blend with preserved ginger, to taste, until very fine, then pass through a fine sieve. Scoop flesh out of rockmelon and blend until fine, then add kirsch to taste and pass through a fine sieve. If the melon purées are not as sweet as you would like, add some castor sugar while you blend. Pour the purées into 3 separate trays, freeze, scratch (see Lavender Granita for method) and serve in layers.→

Lemon granita

1 cup Sugar Syrup (see page 179)
1 cup water
½ cup strained lemon juice
grated zest of ½ lemon

Combine Sugar Syrup with water, lemon juice and zest. Freeze, scratch (see Lavender Granita for method) and serve.

Pink gin granita

½ cup gin
1 cup Sugar Syrup (see page 179)
1 cup water
2½ teaspoons strained lime juice
1 teaspoon Angostura bitters

Combine gin, Sugar Syrup, water, lime juice and bitters. Freeze, scratch (see Lavender Granita for method) and serve.

Raspberry granita

2 cups water
500 g fresh raspberries, frozen overnight,
    or 500 g frozen raspberries
1 cup Sugar Syrup (see page 179)

Mix half the water with the raspberries. Squeeze raspberries with fingers to break down well, then pass through a fine sieve. Mix solids with remaining water and pass through sieve again. Add Sugar Syrup to liquid. Freeze, scratch (see Lavender Granita for method) and serve.

✱ To get lots of juice out of berries, freeze them before passing them through the sieve. Berries oxidise very quickly on contact with metal, so use a stainless steel sieve, or pass them through very quickly.

Clockwise from left: Raspberry granita; Watermelon, honeydew melon & rockmelon granitas; Lemon granita; & Lavender granita

Strawberry ice-cream

Serves 12
9 egg yolks
1 cup castor sugar
3 cups 35%-fat cream
1 kg strawberries,* washed and hulled
½ cup Grand Marnier*

❋ You can omit the strawberries and Grand Marnier and add other fruit purées and appropriate liqueurs of your choice, such as pears and Poire William, apples and calvados, or raspberries and framboise.

Strawberry ice-cream must be the most popular ice-cream after vanilla. If strawberries are one of your favourite flavours, this ice-cream makes a wonderful dessert accompanied by some baked strawberries (see page 125) and a crisp biscuit.

Whisk yolks with ¾ cup of the sugar until pale. Bring cream to the boil in a large saucepan. Pour hot cream into the egg mixture, stirring constantly. Return mixture to the saucepan and stir constantly with a wooden spoon over a low heat until the custard thickens enough to coat the back of the spoon. Make sure that the heat is not too high, or you'll have scrambled eggs instead of custard. Strain into a bowl that's sitting in ice and stir until cool. Refrigerate until well chilled.

Blend the strawberries with the remaining sugar and the Grand Marnier. Fold strawberries into the cold custard, churn in an ice-cream machine and freeze.

Parfait is, in simple terms, ice-cream made without an ice-cream machine. The name comes from the French word for 'perfect', and this simple ice is a perfect accompaniment to many desserts. Each of the following parfait recipes serves 6.

Basic vanilla parfait

100 g white sugar
¼ cup water
6 egg yolks
1½ cups 35%-fat cream, whipped
seeds from ½ vanilla bean or ¼ teaspoon
    vanilla extract (see page 172)

✷ It is important to add the sugar syrup to the whisked egg whites as soon as it is ready. If you delay, it will continue cooking past the desired consistency.

You can use this basic recipe to create an endless variety of flavoured parfaits by omitting the vanilla and adding one of the following: ¼ cup praline (see page 179); 1½ tablespoons strained passionfruit pulp; 1 cup cold espresso coffee (short black); or any fruit purée to taste.

Combine sugar and water in a saucepan, bring to the boil, then simmer until a drop of the syrup forms a soft ball when dropped into cold water.

At the same time, whisk egg yolks in an electric mixer until mixture falling from the beaters forms a ribbon-like pattern on top of the mixture for a few seconds. *Slowly* add sugar syrup to the eggs, drizzling it down the side of the bowl rather than pouring it straight into the middle, whisking all the time. Continue whisking until egg mixture is cool. Fold cream into egg mixture, add vanilla and freeze.

Black sapote parfait with mango & lime

500 g very ripe black sapotes✷
1 quantity Basic Vanilla Parfait (see above),
    unfrozen
1 lime
1 cup Sugar Syrup (see page 179)
3 mangoes, peeled and thinly sliced

✷ Black sapote is a relative of the persimmon, and is also known as black persimmon or chocolate pudding fruit. Like the persimmon, it must be very ripe and squashy to be edible. Shops tend to sell sapotes underripe, as they are easier to handle this way, so you'll need to buy them in advance and ripen them at home for a few days.

Peel sapotes, then cut in half and press through a fine sieve to make about 250 g sapote purée. Fold purée into Basic Vanilla Parfait and freeze in a loaf tin lined with plastic film.

To make candied lime peel, peel the zest from the lime, avoiding the white pith, and slice as thinly as possible. Blanch (see page 174) in boiling water a few times until it doesn't taste too bitter. Drain. Place in a small saucepan with Sugar Syrup and bring to the boil, then reduce heat to low and simmer until thick and syrupy, for about 1 hour. Set aside to cool. Segment the lime (see page 174) and pour with juice over cooled lime peel and Sugar Syrup. Set aside.

Cut sapote parfait into 6 slices and place on serving plates. Arrange overlapping slices of mango at one side of the parfait then drizzle over lime segments, peel and syrup.➔

Egg white parfait

3 egg whites
¾ cup castor sugar
⅓ cup water
300 ml thickened cream
¼ teaspoon vanilla extract (see page 172)

✳ It is important to add the sugar syrup to the whisked egg whites as soon as it is ready. If you delay, it will continue cooking past the desired consistency.

I recently developed this very simple and basic ice-cream for home cooking to use up some egg whites I had left over after making mayonnaise. You can, of course, use the same number of whole eggs for a richer result, but I was amused by the light texture of this parfait, which reminded me of commercial ice-cream.

In an electric mixer, beat egg whites until mixture forms soft peaks, then slowly sprinkle in 1 tablespoon of the sugar, beating all the time. Continue beating until the mixture forms stiff peaks.

At the same time, combine remaining sugar with the water in a small saucepan. Bring to the boil and simmer until a drop of the syrup forms a soft ball when dropped into cold water. As soon as the sugar syrup reaches this stage,✳ *slowly* pour it into the beaten egg whites while whisking constantly, drizzling it down the side of the bowl rather than pouring it straight into the middle, whisking all the time. Continue whisking until mixture is lukewarm, then transfer to another bowl.

In the first bowl (you don't even need to wash the whisk or bowl between egg whites and cream), whisk cream and vanilla extract until soft peaks form. Gently fold cream into egg white mixture until well blended. Freeze until firm.

Sorbets are traditionally sweeter than granitas, and have a lower fruit content. They are also churned in an ice-cream machine, giving them a smooth, rather than icy, texture. The following sorbet recipes all serve 6.

Rose petal & champagne sorbet with praline cream horns

2 cups Sugar Syrup (see page 179)
50 g red, perfumed rose petals (from about 6 large roses)*
3 cups champagne*
champagne, extra, to serve

Praline cream horns

½ cup egg whites
½ cup castor sugar
¾ cup plain flour
125 g unsalted butter, melted
3 tablespoons Hazelnut Praline (see page 179)
¼ quantity Pastry Cream (see page 179)
1 tablespoon icing sugar

✳ Mr Lincoln roses are the only ones with the right colour and perfume for this dish. You can also serve with sugared rose petals (as in the photo overleaf): dip the petals in beaten egg white, toss in castor sugar and leave overnight. You will need 2 bottles of champagne for this recipe.

You'll need to make this sorbet the day before you want to serve it, as the alcohol content means it takes a long time to freeze completely.

To make the rose petal sorbet, combine Sugar Syrup and rose petals and bring to the boil. Remove from heat and leave at room temperature for a few hours, or overnight, to extract most of the perfume, then pass syrup through a sieve, squeezing petals to extract as much syrup as possible. Discard petals. Measure the syrup: you'll need about 1½ cups. Mix with the 3 cups champagne and churn in an ice-cream machine. Freeze overnight.

To make the praline cream horns, mix egg whites with sugar. Sift over flour and fold in. Add melted butter and mix well to incorporate. Refrigerate until cold. Place ½ teaspoon mixture onto a non-stick tray or a baking tray lined with baking paper, and spread into a very thin 8 cm disc. Repeat with remaining mixture – you'll probably need 2 trays, with about 6 discs per tray. Leave trays to rest for 30 minutes at room temperature.

Preheat oven to 150°C. Bake discs for a few minutes, until golden brown. Remove trays from oven and immediately fold each disc into a cone shape (an extra pair of hands is helpful at this stage, as the discs cool quickly and soon become too brittle to shape). Store horns in an airtight container with kitchen paper between the layers.

Fold 2 tablespoons of the Hazelnut Praline into the Pastry Cream and pipe a little of the mixture into each of the horns (if you don't have a piping bag, use a freezer bag with the corner snipped off). Sprinkle remaining praline over the Pastry Cream. Arrange filled cones on a clean surface and sift over icing sugar.

Scoop 1 nicely shaped tablespoon of sorbet into a martini glass or wide champagne flute and place in the centre of a serving plate. Arrange 2 praline cream horns on each serving plate and pour extra ice-cold champagne over the sorbet at the table.➔

Lychee sorbet

750 g strained lychee purée (from about
    1.5 kg whole lychees)
300 ml Sugar Syrup (see page 179)
strained lime juice, to taste

Combine lychee purée with Sugar Syrup and lime juice to taste (about 2 teaspoons). Churn in an ice-cream machine and freeze. Pineapple sorbet can be made using the same method.

Pink grapefruit & Campari sorbet

1 litre strained pink grapefruit juice
100 ml Campari
¾ cup Sugar Syrup (see page 179)
½ teaspoon Angostura bitters

Combine grapefruit juice, Campari, Sugar Syrup and bitters, and churn in an ice-cream machine.

Bellini sorbet

⅔ cup castor sugar
1 cup prosecco*
1 kg white peaches
⅓ cup strained lemon juice
300 g glucose*

* Prosecco is a sparkling wine from the Veneto region of Italy. There seems to be an enormous amount of glucose in this recipe, but after lots of testing we decided that this amount gave the best texture.

This recipe is proof that with wonderful ingredients it doesn't take much to create a masterpiece. The original Bellini was created at Harry's Bar in Venice, where they squeezed perfectly ripe white peaches (never yellow) with their hands to extract the juice, and then passed it through a fine sieve. This is my version, which I first made for this sorbet. I later decided to make the peach purée for the bar at MG Garage and top it with prosecco when guests ordered Bellinis.

Stir sugar into prosecco. Blanch (see page 174) and peel peaches, retaining the skin and placing it in the lemon juice. Chop the peaches and mix into the prosecco. Press peel and lemon juice through a fine sieve to extract as much of the peaches' pink skin colour as possible, then combine this liquid with the prosecco mixture. Process the mixture until very smooth, then stir in glucose,* churn in an ice-cream machine and freeze. This sorbet can be served with slices of peeled peach and with extra prosecco poured over.

Opposite: Rose petal & champagne sorbet with praline cream horns

Framboise + mascarpone mousse with raspberries + sponge fingers

Serves 6
¼ cup framboise*
350 g mascarpone
1 egg
2 egg yolks
⅓ cup white sugar
2 tablespoons water
3 punnets raspberries
2–3 tablespoons icing sugar, to taste
icing sugar, extra, to serve

Sponge fingers
3 eggs, separated
100 g castor sugar
grated zest of 1 lemon
1 egg white
60 g plain flour
½ cup icing sugar

✱ Framboise is a French raspberry liqueur. It is important to add the sugar syrup to the whisked egg whites as soon as it is ready. If you delay, it will continue cooking past the desired consistency. If you want to pipe the mousse into the glasses but don't have a piping bag and nozzle, simply put the mousse in a freezer bag and cut off the corner.

My best lunch ever was at Alain Ducasse in Paris. We had the seafood menu, which was a wonderful experience, and finished with a crème-fraîche-like dessert topped with wild strawberries and a wild strawberry sauce. I was so taken by the flavours of that simple but spectacular dessert served in a martini glass that, on my return, I created a dish to remind me of the experience. My other great memory of that meal is that as we were leaving the restaurant, the waiter came and asked, 'Would you like a loaf of bread to take with you?' Oh, what a wonderful gesture! Two years later we were back at the new Alain Ducasse at Hotel Plaza Athénée. We had a lovely meal, as expected, and at the end I asked the waiter if I could possibly take a menu. 'Not a problem,' he replied. 'As you go out you get the menu, you get the bread, you get the brochure, you get the lot.' The wonderful gesture I remembered had turned into a show bag!

Combine framboise with mascarpone until mixture is soft. Beat egg and egg yolks until pale. At the same time, combine sugar and water in a small saucepan and boil until a drop of the syrup forms a soft ball when dropped into cold water. As soon as the sugar syrup reaches this stage,* *slowly* add it to the eggs, drizzling it down the side of the bowl rather than pouring it straight into the middle, whisking all the time. Continue whisking until egg mixture is cool. Fold mascarpone mixture into egg mixture. Refrigerate.

To make the sponge fingers, preheat oven to 125°C then beat together egg yolks, two-thirds of the castor sugar and all of the lemon zest until pale and fluffy. Whisk all the egg whites until they form soft peaks, then slowly add the remaining castor sugar, whisking until mixture forms stiff peaks. Sift flour over the yolk mixture then fold in gently. Gently fold egg whites into the yolk mixture. Pipe into 10 cm long fingers on a buttered and floured tray. Dust liberally with the icing sugar, leave for 5 minutes then bake for 15 minutes. Reduce oven heat to 100°C and cook for a further 30–40 minutes, or until biscuits are very dry. Cool on a wire rack.

Meanwhile, pick through the raspberries to select 1 cup of the damaged ones, and push these through a fine sieve to make a purée. Add the 2–3 tablespoons icing sugar to taste and mix well.

Spoon or pipe* the framboise & mascarpone mousse into 6 martini glasses, leaving enough space at the top for the whole raspberries. Smooth the top of the mousse. Into each glass, pour 1 tablespoon raspberry purée to cover the surface of the mousse then arrange raspberries on top and dust with extra icing sugar. Dust sponge fingers with more icing sugar and serve 2 or 3 beside each glass.

Passionfruit floating islands with passionfruit tapioca + sugared almonds

Serves 6
¼ cup strained passionfruit pulp*
200 ml egg whites (see page 172)
pinch salt
pinch cream of tartar*
180 g castor sugar
¼ cup strained passionfruit pulp, extra

Passionfruit curd
¼ cup passionfruit pulp, including seeds
3 large eggs, lightly beaten
½ cup castor sugar
60 g unsalted butter, cut into cubes

Passionfruit tapioca
¼ cup tapioca
2 cups milk
½ cup passionfruit curd, from above
¼ cup water

Crème anglaise
7 egg yolks
⅓ cup castor sugar
2 cups milk
1 small vanilla bean, split

Sugared almonds
60 g castor sugar
1½ tablespoons water
60 g flaked almonds

✱ As with berries, you can extract more pulp from passionfruit if you freeze them first. If you have a copper bowl for whisking egg whites, you can omit the cream of tartar from the recipe. Spray-on oil is ideal for greasing the moulds; that way you won't have bits of melted butter left on the meringue islands.

Floating islands are islands of meringue in a sea of custard – they are also called snow eggs or œufs à la neige. This is an example of a relatively simple dessert, that, over the years, I have made increasingly complicated with additions of this and that. I was always fascinated as a child watching the women whisking egg whites for meringues with 2 forks – a whisk was a luxury for a small kitchen! You'll need to start this dessert a few hours ahead of time in order to soak the tapioca. You'll also need to test the recipe before attempting it for your next dinner party. The cooking time will vary from oven to oven, so the first time you try, experiment with several different cooking times. The texture should be very light and smooth, and not at all rubbery. The meringues should rise about 2 cm above the rim when cooked, then sink back down to the level of the rim as they cool; if they sink much lower, it means your oven was too hot and they are overcooked. With meringues, undercooking is always better than overcooking.

To make the passionfruit curd, combine all ingredients in a bowl over a saucepan of boiling water and whisk vigorously until curd starts to thicken. Remove from heat and whisk for 1–2 minutes longer, until mixture cools slightly. Pass curd through a fine sieve to remove seeds. Refrigerate until required.

To make the passionfruit tapioca, soak tapioca in milk for a few hours or overnight. Cook soaked tapioca and milk, covered, in a saucepan over very low heat until tapioca pearls are soft and translucent, about 1 hour. Strain and rinse in a sieve under cold water. Mix passionfruit curd and water through cold tapioca and refrigerate until required.

To make the crème anglaise, whisk egg yolks with half the sugar until pale. Combine milk, vanilla bean and remaining sugar in a small saucepan and bring to the boil. Slowly pour hot milk into egg mixture, whisking constantly. Return mixture to the saucepan and stir constantly with a wooden spoon over a low heat until the custard thickens enough to coat the back of the spoon. Make sure that the heat is not too high or you'll have scrambled eggs instead of custard. Strain into a bowl over ice and stir until cool. Refrigerate until required.

To make the sugared almonds, preheat oven to 150°C then combine sugar and water in a small saucepan over a low heat until sugar dissolves. Remove from heat and stir through almonds. Pour the mixture into a tray lined with greased baking paper, spreading out the nuts so they don't all stick together. Bake for about 15 minutes, stirring every few minutes so that the syrup crystallises on the nuts, until you have dried out clusters of lightly toasted sugared almonds. Cool on the tray.➔

Increase oven temperature to 170°C. Place strained passionfruit pulp in a small saucepan and bring to the boil. Boil until reduced to 1 tablespoon then set aside to cool. Beat egg whites, salt and cream of tartar in an electric mixer on medium speed until the mixture forms soft peaks. Add a third of the sugar and continue beating until the mixture forms firm peaks. Add remaining sugar and beat for another 2–3 minutes until smooth and shiny. Fold through reduced and cooled passionfruit pulp. Spoon into lightly greased* coffee cups and level off with a spatula. Place in a deep bain-marie (see page 174) with hot water reaching halfway up the sides of the cups; the walls of the bain-marie must be higher than the coffee cups and also leave enough room for the meringues to rise. Cover the bain-marie tightly with foil. Bake for 15 minutes. Remove from the oven and leave in bain-marie to cool until required (this can be up until the next day). Do not refrigerate.

Place a 1 cm high disc of passionfruit tapioca in the centre of each of 6 soup plates – it should be just wider than the top of the coffee cups. Carefully unmould the 'islands' from the coffee cups onto the tapioca discs. Pour crème anglaise around them, drizzle over extra passionfruit pulp and scatter with sugared almonds.

Using leftovers

Leftover passionfruit curd is wonderful on toast for breakfast, or can be used to fill tartlet shells to serve as petits fours. Crème anglaise is a basic pouring custard, and is often served with poached fruits, pies and puddings. Store any leftover sugared almonds in an airtight container with baking or grease-proof paper between the layers.

Cumquat Sussex pond pudding with sherry sabayon sauce

Serves 8

500 g self-raising flour
250 g clean suet,* finely chopped
pinch salt
½ cup milk
½ cup water
16 large cumquats, halved, seeds removed
⅔ cup dark brown sugar
160 g unsalted butter
⅓ cup cumquat, or bitter orange, marmalade

Sherry sabayon sauce

8 × 65 g egg yolks
½ cup castor sugar
2 cups milk
1 small vanilla bean, split
¼ cup dry sherry*

✱ Clean suet is available in butcher shops. Sabayon sauce can also be made using calvados or champagne instead of sherry.

Sussex pond pudding comes from Sussex in England, and is traditionally made as a large pudding encasing one whole lemon. Gay Bilson had it on the menu at Berowra Waters Inn; it tasted delicious but fell apart when it was cut for serving. So I created this version, making individual puddings and using cumquats instead of a lemon.

Start sauce by whisking egg yolks with sugar until well mixed. Combine milk and split vanilla bean in a small saucepan and bring to the boil. Gradually add hot milk (with vanilla bean) to yolk mixture, whisking constantly to combine. Return mixture to saucepan and cook over a medium heat, stirring constantly with a wooden spoon, until mixture thickens just enough to coat the back of the spoon. Strain into a bowl that's sitting in ice and keep whisking until cold. Remove the vanilla bean, but scrape the seeds into the cold custard and stir through. Refrigerate until required.

Combine flour, suet and salt in a food processor and pulse until the mixture resembles fine breadcrumbs. Add milk and water and pulse until mixture forms a firm dough. Knead dough until smooth. Roll out half the pastry on a floured surface to a thickness of 6 mm. Butter 8 × ½ cup moulds (or coffee cups) liberally. Cut 8 discs from the pastry, using one of the moulds as a guide. Combine the pastry off-cuts with the remaining pastry and divide into 8 balls. Roll out each ball into a circle 6 mm thick and use to line the moulds. Divide cumquats, brown sugar, butter and marmalade among the moulds. Wet the inside edge of the pastry at the top of the moulds, place the pastry discs on top to form lids and pinch well to seal. Cover the top of each mould with a little plastic film, then cover with foil to seal tightly. Place puddings in a steamer for 1 hour.

Unmould puddings onto soup plates. Place cold custard for the sauce in a wide saucepan, stir in sherry and whisk vigorously over high heat until hot and frothy. Remove from heat and pour over puddings, whisking all the while to avoid the sauce curdling at the bottom of the pan. Serve immediately.

Amaretto cake with caramelised figs

Serves 8

5 × 65 g eggs, separated
¾ cup castor sugar
100 ml amaretto*
1 tablespoon finely grated lemon zest
2 egg whites (from 65 g eggs)
pinch cream of tartar*
150 g plain flour
pinch salt
100 g Clarified Butter (see page 175), melted
½ cup Sugar Syrup (see page 179)
½ cup amaretto, extra
16 ripe soft-skinned figs
2 cups castor sugar
2 tablespoons icing sugar

* Amaretto is an Italian almond liqueur. If you have a copper bowl for whisking egg whites, you can omit the cream of tartar from the recipe.

'A good cake never sinks in the middle,' they say. The inspiration for this cake came from Alice Waters' wonderful olive oil and Sauternes cake. As delicious as it tasted, though, it still had a tendency to sink in the middle when I tried to make it (through no fault of the recipe, I'm sure). I decided to adapt the idea and make a cake using clarified butter and amaretto. I had some success with the recipe, but before I had fully mastered it, I foolishly agreed to teach it at a cooking class. I made one cake on the morning of the class, which, being cooked in a different oven from the one I was used to, failed miserably. During the class I demonstrated the mixing of the cake, explaining that the version I'd made earlier for them to taste wasn't quite right, but encouraging them to persevere at home to perfect the technique. In my annoyance over the failure, I turned the oven off earlier than I should have and completely forgot about the demonstration cake left in the oven until the following day, when I returned to prepare for the next class. To my surprise, I found it still in the oven and risen to perfection! It seems the slow cooling in the oven was the secret to the perfect cake.

Preheat oven to 150°C. Butter a 20 cm springform cake tin and line the sides and bottom with baking paper, making sure the paper rises half as high again above the cake tin. Butter and flour the baking paper.

Beat the egg yolks with half the sugar until mixture falling from the beaters forms a ribbon-like pattern on top of the mixture for a few seconds. Gradually whisk in the 100 ml amaretto and lemon zest. Whisk all the egg whites with cream of tartar until the mixture forms soft peaks. Gradually add remaining sugar, beating until the mixture forms firm peaks. Fold a third of the egg white mixture into the egg yolk mixture. Sift flour and salt over the yolk mixture, spread remaining egg white mixture on top, and gently fold all together. Mix a generous tablespoonful of the egg mixture into the Clarified Butter, then fold the butter mixture back into the egg mixture. Pour into the cake tin and bake for 30 minutes. Reduce oven temperature to 130°C and bake for a further 30 minutes. Turn oven off and leave cake to cool in the oven.

Combine Sugar Syrup and extra amaretto and pour over the cooled cake.

Just before serving, preheat oven to 220°C. Dip figs in water, then roll in castor sugar. Spread out in a single layer in a baking dish and bake for 10–15 minutes, until sugar caramelises.

Cut cake into 8 slices and sift icing sugar over each slice. Place a slice of cake on each plate and serve 2 hot figs and their juices on the side.

Flourless banana cake

Serves 6

250 g whole almonds, blanched
    (see page 174) and skinned
2 eggs
125 g castor sugar
½ teaspoon baking powder
2 teaspoons bitter almonds* (optional)
250 g bananas, peeled
2 teaspoons strained lemon juice
½ cup flaked almonds
1 tablespoon icing sugar, to serve
1 cup 45%-fat cream, to serve

✱ Bitter almonds are available in Asian and Chinese grocery shops. To make a neat edge for a perfect slice, cut through the nuts and the top layer of the cake using a pair of scissors, then cut out slices using a knife.

My business partner at MG Garage, Greg Duncan, loves bananas, so during the 5 years the restaurant was open, we did everything we could with them: soufflés and ice-creams, baked and caramelised. So what to do for his 50th birthday? I finally came up with this light, moist, flourless cake and served 50 small versions, each topped with a banana covered in pink jelly. You'll need about 3 large bananas for this recipe – very ripe bananas are best. The cake is best eaten the day it's made, while the almond flakes on top are still crisp – they will have gone soft by the next day.

Preheat oven to 150°C. Toast skinned almonds on a baking tray in the oven for about 20 minutes or until golden and leave aside to cool. Leave the oven on at 150°C.

Butter a 22 cm fluted flan tin (with removable base) and line with baking paper; wetting the baking paper and squeezing it well to remove the moisture will make it more pliable, so that it fits the fluted tin better. Grease the paper with more butter.

Beat the eggs with the sugar for about 10 minutes, or until mixture falling from the beaters forms a ribbon-like pattern on top of the mixture for a few seconds. Meanwhile, grind the almonds, baking powder and bitter almonds (if using) to a fine meal in a food processor (do not over-grind or they will become moist and sticky). Dust the tin with about 2 tablespoons of the almond meal then fold the remaining almond meal into the egg mixture. Purée the bananas with the lemon juice and fold immediately into the cake mixture – bananas must be puréed at the last minute to prevent them going black. Pour the mixture into the prepared cake tin and scatter the surface with flaked almonds. Bake for about 40 minutes, until a skewer comes out clean. Remove from oven and leave to cool in tin.

When cool, sift over icing sugar, cut into slices* and serve immediately with a dollop of thick cream on the side.

Pink grapefruit peel + almond tart

Serves 8
100 g whole almonds, blanched
    (see page 174) and skinned
1 teaspoon chopped bitter almonds*
50 g unsalted butter
⅓ cup icing sugar
1 egg, lightly beaten
2 teaspoons dark rum
1 tablespoon plain flour

Candied grapefruit peel
2 large pink grapefruits
400 g castor sugar
1 cup water

Sable pastry
125 g unsalted butter, softened
⅓ cup icing sugar, sifted
1 large egg yolk (or 2 small egg yolks)
grated zest of 1 lemon
160 g plain flour
small pinch salt

✱ Bitter almonds are available in Asian or
Chinese grocery shops.

Candied grapefruit peel is a staple petit four in many restaurants, and one of my favourites. In this recipe I cook the peel as for petits fours, but not as dry, and use it as a topping for an almond tart – it's a delicious combination.

Make candied grapefruit peel by cutting grapefruit in half and squeezing the juice for later use (in a sorbet or granita). Cut each half into 16 wedges then place wedges in a saucepan and cover with cold water. Bring to the boil, drain and repeat blanching 6–8 times, until the peel no longer tastes bitter. Put grapefruit peel in a saucepan with sugar and water, and cook over a very, very low heat for 1½–2 hours, until peel has absorbed most of the syrup. Allow peel to cool in the syrup before draining and using. Reserve syrup for glazing tart.

To make the sable pastry, beat butter with icing sugar, using a wooden spoon, until soft. Add egg yolk and lemon zest and mix well. Sift flour and salt over butter mixture, then mix until just combined – don't over-mix. Refrigerate dough until cold.

Preheat oven to 150°C. Toast the almonds on a baking tray in the oven for about 20 minutes or until golden, and leave aside to cool. Increase oven temperature to 175°C. Grind cooled almonds with bitter almonds in a food processor. Beat butter with icing sugar, using a wooden spoon, until well combined. Combine beaten egg with rum then add to butter and sugar mixture a little at a time. Stir in almond meal. Sift over flour and stir to combine. Refrigerate until cold.

Roll pastry out thinly on a floured surface and place in a 20–22 cm fluted tart tin with a removable base. Refrigerate until cold. Fill cold tart shell with cold almond mixture and arrange candied grapefruit peel on top. Bake for 20 minutes then cover with foil to avoid grapefruit drying out and bake for a further 20–30 minutes, until pastry is golden brown.

Leave at room temperature until cold then brush over some syrup from the candied grapefruit peel to glaze. Use a serrated knife to cut carefully through the peel.

Cardamom yoghurt pudding + saffron pears

Serves 6
4 leaves gelatine (see page 172)
200 ml 35%-fat cream
100 g castor sugar
¼ teaspoon vanilla extract (see page 172)
¼ teaspoon ground cardamom seeds
600 ml plain yoghurt*

Saffron pears
2 cups castor sugar
3 cups water
3 cups fruity white wine
¼ teaspoon saffron threads
6 pears, peeled, halved and cored

* You'd expect me to use Greek yoghurt for this recipe, but I've found the basic plain supermarket yoghurt works best. Different yoghurts will have different setting points; if you feel the puddings have set too firmly, leave them to come to room temperature before serving.

I first came across a buttermilk pudding when Damien Pignolet and Mogens Bay Esbensen made one at Butler's restaurant. That recipe did the rounds of the restaurants for many years and even still appears on some menus. With Damien's and Mogens' influence the pudding had a decidedly northern European flavour. For my part, I used my Greek heritage and made it with yoghurt, and, at different times, have flavoured it with cardamom, rose geranium, vanilla and saffron. I served this dish, flavoured with rose geranium leaves and accompanied by Grand Marnier-soaked strawberries, for 3 consecutive years at the Sydney Food & Wine Fair in Hyde Park. It was so popular that we sold 500 serves within an hour every time.

Soak gelatine in 1 cup cold water for 2–3 minutes. Combine half the cream with the sugar in a small saucepan over a low heat until the mixture just boils and the sugar is dissolved. Meanwhile, whip the remaining cream with the vanilla and ground cardamom seeds and refrigerate until required. Squeeze gelatine gently to remove as much water as possible, then add to heated cream and stir over a low heat until completely dissolved. Remove from heat, add half the yoghurt and stir to combine. Stir heated cream mixture into remaining yoghurt in a bowl that's sitting in a larger bowl of ice. Whisk mixture over ice until very cold and starting to thicken. Gently fold in the spiced whipped cream. Rinse 6 × ½ cup dariole moulds (or coffee cups) in cold water and shake to remove excess. Divide yoghurt mixture among the moulds, smooth tops and refrigerate until set.

To make the saffron pears, place sugar in a small non-aluminium saucepan with water, wine and saffron. Bring to the boil and add pears, then reduce heat, cover sauce-pan with a piece of dampened baking paper and a lid, and cook just below simmering for about 30 minutes or until pears are tender. Reserve 2 cups of the poaching liquid, leaving pears in remaining liquid to cool. Refrigerate when cool. Boil reserved poaching liquid until reduced to ½ cup.

Unmould one pudding on each plate, place 2 pear halves on the side and pour reduced poaching liquid over pudding and pears.

Galaktoboureko

Serves 6

2 cups milk
½ small vanilla bean, split
½ cup castor sugar
¼ cup fine semolina
2 small eggs
30 g unsalted butter
½ cup whole almonds, blanched
    (see page 174) and skinned
1 tablespoon pure icing sugar
¼ teaspoon ground cinnamon
6 × 30 cm sheets Greek Filo Pastry*
    (see page 177)
125 g unsalted butter, melted
spiced orange salad (see page 120),
    to serve

Lemon sugar syrup

2 cups sugar
1 cup water
grated zest of 1 lemon*

* You can use bought filo pastry, but you'll need to use a double thickness, and the finished dish will have a different texture. You can use the zest of ½ orange instead of 1 lemon if you like. The tubes can be assembled and refrigerated the day before they're needed and then baked just before serving.

Galaktoboureko is a Greek custard pie. Traditionally, a custard is made on the stove top and poured onto commercial filo pastry in a large tray, topped with more filo, baked to cook the custard, then removed from the oven and doused in sugar syrup. I always found that this method resulted in soggy pastry, especially on the bottom. I'm not trying to reinvent traditional Greek cooking, but at MG Garage I made my own filo pastry and used cooked custard, which gives a drier and crisper pastry and a custard that's still moist in the middle. Once my Galaktoboureko comes out of the oven, I soak it in sugar syrup for just a minute then serve it hot, so that it remains crisp. You'll need to make the custard several hours before assembling the pastries.

Preheat oven to 165°C. Combine milk, vanilla bean and half the sugar in a saucepan and bring to the boil. Sprinkle semolina into the hot milk and return to the boil, stirring constantly. Remove mixture from heat once it boils, and stir for 30 seconds as it thickens. Whisk together eggs and remaining sugar. Pour hot milk and semolina mixture into the eggs, stirring constantly. Add butter and stir until combined. Pour into a buttered 12 × 15 cm ceramic or Pyrex baking dish. Cover with a lid or tray, to avoid a skin forming on the custard, making sure the baking dish is deep enough for the custard not to touch the lid when it puffs up. Bake for 30–40 minutes, until a thin skewer comes out clean. Remove baked custard from oven, allow to cool a little, then refrigerate until cold. Reduce oven temperature to 150°C.

Meanwhile, toast the almonds on a baking tray in the oven for about 20 minutes or until golden. Leave aside to cool, then chop finely and mix with icing sugar and cinnamon.

When custard is cold, turn it out of the dish and cut into 6 large fingers (about 12 × 2.5 × 2.5 cm). Brush filo pastry sheets very generously with melted butter and sprinkle over two-thirds of the almond mixture. Place a finger of custard at one end of each sheet and roll up in the pastry, forming a pastry tube with a custard centre. Brush tubes liberally with butter, sprinkle over remaining almond mixture and refrigerate until cold.*

To make the lemon sugar syrup, combine all ingredients in a small saucepan, bring to the boil, then remove from heat and keep warm.

Preheat oven to 200°C. Bake tubes for 10–20 minutes, until golden. Remove from oven then place straight into the warm lemon sugar syrup for 30 seconds, or pour the syrup over them. Arrange some orange salad on each serving plate. Cut each tube in half diagonally and place on top of salad. Serve immediately.

Blood plum + blackcurrant pies with cassis sauce

Serves 6

6 blood plums,* each cut into 6 wedges
6 tablespoons blackcurrants*
1 teaspoon 35%-fat cream
2 egg yolks, beaten
6 tablespoons 45%-fat cream

Self-raising shortcrust pastry

200 g plain flour
1½ tablespoons castor sugar
1½ teaspoons baking powder
100 g cold butter
¼ cup iced water

Marzipan

100 g whole almonds, blanched, skinned
    and toasted (see page 174)
50 g butter
2 tablespoons pure icing sugar
1 tablespoon amaretto*

Cassis sauce

125 g blackcurrants
½ cup crème de cassis*
100 ml Sugar Syrup (see page 179)

✳ When plums have been out of season,
I've made these pies using half a sliced
pear per pie. Fresh blackcurrants have
a very short season, so thawed frozen
blackcurrants can be used. Amaretto is an
Italian almond liqueur. Crème de cassis is a
sweet, red, blackcurrant-flavoured liqueur.

I learnt to make this type of shortcrust pastry using the bramble cake recipe of Stephanie Alexander's grandmother. The original pastry was made with self-raising flour and lard, and seemed indestructible. I have changed it over the years, and now use butter instead of lard and a combination of plain flour and baking powder instead of self-raising flour.

To make the pastry, sift flour, sugar and baking powder together into a mixing bowl. Grate in butter, add water, and knead into a smooth ball – don't overwork it. Rest pastry 30 minutes. Roll out half the pastry on a lightly floured surface to about 2 mm thickness. Cut out 6 × 10 cm circles, preferably with a fluted cutter, and refrigerate until required. Add off-cuts to the remaining pastry, divide into 6 balls and refrigerate until required.

To make the marzipan, combine all ingredients in a food processor until the mixture forms a smooth paste.

Make the cassis sauce by thoroughly blending all ingredients in a blender or food processor and straining through a fine sieve. Keep at room temperature.

Remove one of the 6 pastry balls from the fridge and roll into a 15 cm circle. Place on a baking tray lined with baking paper. Divide marzipan into 6 then flatten 1 piece in the palm of your hand and place in the centre of the pastry. Lay 4 pieces of plum on the marzipan to form a square, then 1 tablespoon blackcurrants on the marzipan in the centre of the plum square. Place 2 plum pieces on top of the blackcurrants, skin-side up. Neatly fold pastry over the top of the filling, pleating around the plums to form an open pie. Combine 35%-fat cream and egg yolks then brush lightly over the edges of the pastry. Place a 10 cm pastry circle on top of the pie, pressing it lightly over the pleats. Brush lightly with egg yolk mixture and refrigerate. Repeat with remaining ingredients, so that you have 6 pies. Leave them to rest in the fridge for 30 minutes before baking.

Preheat oven to 200°C. Bake pies for 12–15 minutes until golden. Ladle a little cassis sauce onto each plate, place a pie in the centre of the sauce and 45%-fat cream on the side.

Petits fours

'Petits fours' is the French term for the scrumptious little morsels that restaurants serve with tea and coffee. They can be as simple as biscotti or as complex as any dessert. One of the most popular petits fours at MG Garage, and one that doesn't require much work, was a fruit tartlet. You can buy very good small tart shells and pastry cream from good pastry shops (or use the Pastry Cream recipe on page 179), then all you need are a few slices of fruit (berries are good) and some redcurrant jelly to melt as a glaze. Cherry Tomato & Almond Preserve (see page 168) also makes a great topping.

Ancient Greek biscuits

Makes about 40

1 cup slivered almonds

1 cup hazelnuts

2 cups sesame seeds, toasted
  (see page 174)

1 tablespoon bitter almonds,* chopped

1 tablespoon poppy seeds

1½ teaspoons Ras El Hanout
  (see page 177)

200 g honey

* Bitter almonds are available in Asian or Chinese grocery shops.

In *The Classical Cookbook* by Andrew Dalby and Sally Grainger, Chrysippus of Tyana is quoted, describing Cretan cakes called gastris that were made by roasting and pounding sweet and bitter almonds, hazelnuts and poppy seeds with boiled honey and a good quantity of pepper, and sandwiching this paste between a mixture of sesame seeds and honey. Greeks still make a honey and toasted sesame seed biscuit today called pasteli, similar to modern honey nut bars and muesli bars – a reminder that some of today's food has its roots in ancient times. I use Ras El Hanout in this recipe because it's always in my pantry, but you don't need to make it specially; use a good dash of whatever spices you have at hand, as long as you include black pepper. After all, I can't imagine a Greek or Roman cook from thousands of years ago using measuring spoons!

Preheat oven to 150°C. Toast almonds and hazelnuts in the oven (see page 174), on separate trays, until golden. Wrap hazelnuts in a tea towel while they are still very hot, and rub well to remove most of the skin. Chop roughly. Toast sesame seeds in a dry frying pan until golden. While nuts and sesame seeds are still hot, combine with remaining ingredients except honey.

Carefully bring honey to the boil in a small saucepan. Keep boiling until a drop of it forms a soft ball when dropped into cold water (the honey will have thickened and darkened, as if starting to turn into caramel). Mix hot honey into warm nut mixture; if the nut mixture has gone too cold, it will be difficult to mix the honey through it. Spread mixture onto a 30 × 40 cm baking tray lined with baking paper and press down to flatten. Once cool, but not completely cold, turn out onto a chopping board and cut into desired shapes (squares, fingers, diamonds, triangles). Store in an airtight container with baking or greaseproof paper between the layers.

Florentines

Makes 40–60

3 cups slivered almonds
⅓ cup plain flour, sifted
½ cup finely chopped candied orange
1 cup castor sugar
⅔ cup honey
⅔ cup 35%-fat cream
80 g butter
250 g semi-sweet (57%) couverture
　　chocolate (see page 172)

✳ Florentines can be cut into shapes other than triangles or circles, using biscuit cutters. Alternatively, you can leave the biscuit whole, spread it with melted chocolate and then break it into rough shapes. Leftover biscuits can be stored in an airtight container for a few days with baking or greaseproof paper between layers, or frozen until required.

Traditionally, Florentines are large, thick discs. Years ago I developed this more delicate version by rolling the cooked biscuits as thinly as possible between 2 sheets of baking paper. Since then, these are the only Florentines I've served. At MG Garage we served these biscuits with the Coffee Cardamom & Hazelnut Custards (see page 132). You'll need a candy thermometer to make this recipe.

Preheat oven to 150°C. Toast the almonds (see page 174) on a baking tray in the oven for about 10 minutes or until golden. Remove from oven but leave the oven on. Mix almonds with flour and candied orange in a metal bowl. Combine sugar, honey, cream and butter in a saucepan with the candy thermometer and cook over a high heat until mixture reaches 116°C (about 5 minutes after it starts boiling). Pour sugar mixture over nut mixture and stir to combine (careful – the bowl will get very hot).

Pour mixture onto 3 large (30 × 40 cm) baking trays lined with baking paper then spread out as thinly as possible. Bake for about 20 minutes, or until mixture bubbles and the edges are very dark brown. Remove from oven and, with the help of the baking paper, lift one Florentine onto a chopping board. Place another sheet of baking paper on top and roll with a rolling pin to roll the Florentine as thinly as possible. Repeat with the second and third tray of Florentines. Remove the top sheets of baking paper while still warm and use a long knife to trim off any dark edges and to mark the Florentines into triangles.✳ Leave at room temperature to cool, then cut along the marked lines.

Melt chocolate in a bowl over a saucepan of hot but not boiling water (making sure the bowl is not touching the water). Spread melted chocolate onto one side of each biscuit.

Cherry tomato + almond preserve

1.2 kg cherry tomatoes*
1 kg castor sugar
½ cup water
100 g whole almonds, blanched
    (see page 174) and skinned
2 tablespoons strained lemon juice
2 strips lemon zest
1 cinnamon stick
5 cloves

✱ Don't use over-ripe cherry tomatoes for this dish – they need to be quite firm so they don't disintegrate when cooked. You can also make this preserve with large tomatoes – if so, put the almonds inside the tomatoes to keep them plump.

Greeks serve spoon sweets to welcome their guests. As I see it, a quick sugar hit is as energising as a cup of coffee or a refreshing cold drink. Curls of preserved orange peel are common, and I remember as a child helping my mother thread the curls of peel onto strings before she put them into the pot of sugar syrup to be preserved. A popular summer version is a tablespoonful of fondant in a tall glass of iced water. Almost anything can be turned into a spoon sweet, things as diverse as tiny eggplants, green walnuts (before the shells form) and rose petals. This one, using cherry tomatoes and almonds, is one of the more unusual examples. You'll need to start this recipe at least 4 days in advance.

Make a small cross in the skin at the base of each tomato. Plunge tomatoes into boiling water for a few seconds, drain well, then peel off skin. Sprinkle peeled tomatoes with half the sugar. Refrigerate for 24 hours, to allow the sugar to extract the liquid from the tomatoes.

Drain liquid from tomatoes and pour into a saucepan with the water and the remaining sugar. Bring to the boil, reduce heat and simmer for 5 minutes, skimming frequently. Add tomatoes, almonds, lemon juice, lemon zest, cinnamon and cloves. Return to the boil, skim, remove from heat, cool, then refrigerate for 24 hours.

The next day, drain and retain tomatoes and other solids, and boil syrup until it starts to thicken and look jam-like, about 15–20 minutes after boiling. Return tomatoes and other solids to syrup and return to the boil. Remove from heat, pour into sterilised glass jars and allow to cool. Refrigerate for 24 hours.

The next day, check the consistency of your preserve. If it is still too thin, drain off the tomatoes and other solids then bring syrup to the boil for a few more minutes to thicken it. Return tomatoes and other solids to syrup and return to the boil. Remove from heat and return preserve to jars. Allow to cool and then refrigerate until required. It will keep for weeks in the fridge.

Grandma Domna's karidato (walnut turnovers)

Makes 16

250 g plain flour
2 teaspoons pure icing sugar
¼ cup extra-virgin olive oil
60 g unsalted butter
¼ cup warm water
olive oil, for deep-frying
pure icing sugar, extra, for dusting

Filling

60 g unsalted butter
100 g Fresh Breadcrumbs (see page 175)
250 g shelled walnuts, roughly chopped
4 tablespoons pure icing sugar
2 teaspoons ground cinnamon
grated zest of 1 orange
1 egg, lightly beaten
2 tablespoons brandy

✱ Rolling the pastry between sheets of baking paper can help make it as thin as possible. It's important that the icing sugar be dusted over the pastries while they are still hot, to ensure it clings to the pastry. They will remain crisp for a couple of days stored in an airtight container – dust with a little extra icing sugar before serving.

There were always big celebrations in my household in early January. Greeks celebrate 'name days' instead of birthdays, and my father's name day was 6 January, mine is 7 January and Grandma Domna's was 8 January. Another reason to celebrate was that Grandma would make her favourite pastries – a once-a-year treat looked forward to by everyone visiting during the 3 days of celebrations. I wanted to include the recipe here, but was astonished that I couldn't find one in my many Greek cookbooks. The closest I could find were Middle-Eastern recipes for savoury turnovers called sanbusak, or for Indian samosas. Grandma grew up near Istanbul, so there was a lot of Middle-Eastern influence in her cooking. I rang family in Greece, only to discover that Grandma hadn't passed on the recipe to anyone. Cousin Kaliopitsa, a great cook, had a good memory of the filling, although she'd never tried to make the pastries. Brother George offered me the benefit of his experience in pastry-making when he sent me the following. 'Make a pastry from flour, oil and yeast. Cut into walnut-sized chunks and roll into 12 cm discs. Fill with a spoonful of filling, fold and seal, then pan-fry until golden.' He remembered the method, he said, from his days in his 'first job as a pastry cook'. My dear, sweet brother . . . it was his after-school job at the age of 11!

To make the pastry, sift flour with the 2 teaspoons icing sugar into a bowl. Heat oil and butter in a small saucepan until butter is just melted. Pour into flour and combine with a fork until mixture resembles breadcrumbs. Add water and mix with a fork, then knead dough lightly into a ball – do not over-knead. Wrap in plastic film and chill for 1 hour.

To make the filling, melt butter in a frying pan, add breadcrumbs and toast until lightly golden. Remove from heat, add walnuts, icing sugar, cinnamon and orange zest, and mix well. Add the egg and brandy and combine. Refrigerate until firm.

Divide pastry into 16 walnut-sized balls and return to fridge. Divide filling into 16 walnut-sized balls. Squeeze each ball of filling into a semi-circle in the palm of your hand. Return to refrigerator. Remove a pastry ball from the fridge and leave to soften for a few minutes. Dust a large square of baking paper with a little plain flour. Using a small rolling pin, roll the pastry ball into a 12 cm circle.✱ Place filling on one side of pastry circle. Moisten edge of the pastry with a little water, then fold pastry in half to enclose filling. Pinch edges to seal, then fold sealed edge over. Repeat with remaining pastry and filling.

In a deep saucepan, heat olive oil to 180°C (a bread cube will sizzle when added). Fry pastries in batches until golden, about 1 minute each side. Drain on kitchen paper and dust with lots of icing sugar while hot.✱ Allow to cool, then serve at room temperature.

Ingredients

All recipes use salted butter unless otherwise stated. The standard egg size for these recipes is 60 g; 1 × 60 g egg well separated gives 40 ml egg white. All recipes using cream state the fat content of the cream: 35%-fat cream is single or pouring cream; 45%-fat cream is double or thick cream (but not 'thick-ened', which has had gelatine added).

Anchovies – Ortiz brand in oil is best. If, however, you decide to use salted anchovies, soak them in water for 30 minutes to remove excess salt, then dry well.

Candied clementines – you can use other candied citrus instead of clementines. Candied citrus is available from good delicatessens and providores.

Caul fat – also called crepinette, is available from butchers in 50 g or 100 g lots, and keeps well in the freezer.

Cornichons – are baby dill pickles, the size of a little finger.

Couverture chocolate – has a higher cocoa butter content (usually minimum 32%) than normal chocolate, which gives a glossier finish and makes a thinner chocolate shell. To melt chocolate, bring a saucepan of water to the boil then remove from heat. Place chocolate in a bowl over saucepan and leave to melt for 5–10 minutes. Do not allow steam to come into contact with melting chocolate, or chocolate will 'seize' and go grainy. Do not stir chocolate until it has completely melted, as this can also cause it to seize. If chocolate does seize, stirring in a small amount of butter may return it to normal texture.

Dried Greek oregano – also called rigani; the whole stems are dried while in flower, so you use flowers as well as leaves. It's available in Greek delicatessens.

Gelatine – there are different grades of gelatine leaves available: gold, silver, bronze and titanium, gold being the lightest. These recipes use gold grade gelatine. Leaf gelatine is available from good delicatessens and is superior to powdered.

Parmesan cheese – always buy a piece of parmesan and grate it freshly, as pre-grated parmesan goes rancid very quickly.

Vanilla extract – always use vanilla extract, not vanilla essence.

All tablespoon measurements refer to Australian tablespoons – i.e. 20 ml, or 4 teaspoons, and 1 cup is 250 ml. The oven temperatures given in the recipes refer to a fan-forced oven. If your oven is not fan-forced, increase the temperature by 10°C – but experiment and check for your particular oven. If your oven is one of those new super-ovens that hold their temperature, when it comes to reducing the temperature of the oven for a recipe you might have to open the door a little (prop it open with something fireproof) to get the temperature down to the desired level.

After my knives and my pasta machine, my mandoline is the one thing I can't do without in the kitchen. Its razor-sharp blade cuts perfect slices or thin strips, but it's important always to use the guard, or sooner or later you'll cut yourself (every chef has). You can buy mandolines in most homeware shops.

Always keep a supply of muslin, kitchen twine, bamboo skewers, toothpicks, baking paper and other staples on hand in the kitchen.

Basic terms

Bain-marie – (water bath) a vessel containing water in which pots of custard or other delicate items are cooked. The water surrounds the custard with a gentle heat and prevents it from curdling or splitting. It's easy to improvise a bain-marie with an oven-proof dish.

Blanching – involves plunging an ingredient into boiling water for a brief time, then into cold or iced water to stop the cooking process. This technique has a number of uses, depending on the product being blanched.

- almonds – plunge almonds into boiling water for 30 seconds, then drain and rinse under cold water. Squeeze almonds out of their skins. It's worth skinning almonds yourself for any recipe, as they have a better flavour than the commercially skinned ones.
- broad beans – to loosen the outside skin, plunge into boiling water for 30 seconds, then tip into a strainer and rinse with plenty of cold water to stop the cooking process.
- capers – to reduce saltiness, combine 1 cup capers with 2 cups water, boil, drain, discard water. Repeat. Taste; if they still taste too salty, blanch once more.
- citrus zest – to remove bitterness, combine zest of 1 lemon or 1 orange with 2 cups water, boil, drain, discard water. Repeat. Taste; if it still tastes too bitter, blanch once more.
- garlic – to remove raw flavour from garlic slices, plunge them into salted boiling water for a few seconds then refresh in cold water and drain.
- tomatoes – to peel, cut out the stem end of the tomatoes with a small knife, plunge them into boiling water for 30 seconds, then refresh in cold water and the skin should peel off easily. To seed, halve tomatoes horizontally and gently squeeze each half over a sieve placed over a bowl, removing seeds but capturing the juices in the bowl.

- peaches – a perfect peach is easy to peel, but unless you have your own tree, a perfect peach will be almost impossible to find. Score the peach from top to bottom along the groove, then blanch using the same method as for tomatoes. If, however, you want to poach your peaches in sugar syrup, leave the skin on, to give a better colour to the peach and syrup. Remove the skin just before serving.

Butterflied fish – the backbone and rib cage are removed, leaving the head, tail and skin holding the 2 fillets together. The fillets can then be opened out, making a shape resembling a butterfly. This method is mostly used when you want to put stuffing between the fillets.

French trimmed (lamb shanks) – ask your butcher to cut the shank just before the joint and trim the bone of all meat and sinew for about 2.5 cm from the end.

Segmenting citrus fruit – with a small, sharp knife, remove skin and pith from the fruit. Holding the fruit in the palm of your hand, cut along the sides of the white fibres and lift out the clean segment of fruit.

Toasting nuts and seeds – toast nuts on a baking tray in a 150°C oven for 5–20 minutes, depending on the size of the nuts, until golden (pine nuts will take about 5 minutes, whereas almonds will take 15–20 minutes). Stir them every 5 minutes or so to make sure they colour evenly. Nuts can also be toasted in a dry frying pan or with a little vegetable oil over a low heat and stirred constantly until golden. Toast sesame seeds in a dry frying pan until golden, or on an oven tray in a 150°C oven for a few minutes – but watch them closely!

Clarified butter

Melt butter over a very low heat until it just starts to foam. Remove from the heat and set aside to cool, but not set. The milk solids will fall to the bottom and the clarified butter will float to the top. Carefully pour the clarified butter into a clean container, leaving the white milk solids behind. Discard solids and store butter, covered and refrigerated, until required.

If you prefer butter with a nutty flavour, as I do, heat butter in a larger pan (so it's less likely to foam over). Once it foams, continue heating (watching closely as the foam rises very quickly, like boiling milk, and could cause a fire if it overflows). By the time the foam subsides, the milk solids will have turned nut brown. Remove from heat and set aside to cool and separate as above. If you heat the butter beyond the point where the solids turn nut brown, it will taste unpleasant. When a recipe calls for clarified butter you can use ghee (available from supermarkets, Asian grocery shops and health food shops), which has a slightly different flavour but is a perfectly acceptable substitute.

Fresh breadcrumbs

Cut the crusts off day-old white bread and grate or pulse in a food processor until crumbed. Crusts can be left on for a more rustic flavour and texture. Always store fresh breadcrumbs in the freezer, or they will go mouldy.

Gremolata

1 cup finely chopped flat-leaf parsley leaves
1 clove garlic, finely chopped
grated zest of 1 lemon

Combine ingredients thoroughly.

Gremolata breadcrumbs

To my knowledge, Gremolata Breadcrumbs is not a classic recipe – this is just my version of Fresh Breadcrumbs combined with Gremolata.

1 cup Fresh Breadcrumbs (see above)
½ quantity Gremolata (see above)

Combine breadcrumbs and Gremolata thoroughly.

Toasted herb breadcrumbs

60 g unsalted butter
½ cup finely chopped brown onion
½ cup finely chopped celery
1 cup Fresh Breadcrumbs (see above)
1 tablespoon snipped chives
2 teaspoons chopped dill
1 tablespoon chopped flat-leaf parsley leaves
salt, to taste
freshly ground black pepper, to taste

Melt butter in a saucepan, then add onion and celery and fry until well browned (but not burnt). Strain the vegetables from the butter and return butter to saucepan. Fry breadcrumbs in butter until golden and slightly dry. Combine with fried onion and celery, chives, dill, parsley, salt and pepper. Store for 1 week in the fridge, or for up to 3 months in the freezer.

Fish stock

Stock ingredients can be multiplied to make larger quantities, and the excess can be frozen for 3 months in ice-cube trays for easy portion control. This stock will gel on its own. Snapper bones give the best flavour and the most jellied consistency for fish stock; whole snapper can be used for a richer flavour. This stock can make a simple soup with the addition of rice or a few vegetables. One always assumes that a few vegetables and some bones will give a wonderful chicken, meat or fish stock. I recall the story of an apprentice who accidentally swapped around the fish stock and chicken stock in the cool room. The chef used the wrong stock for a week without realising, because the stocks were so weak that they all tasted the same. It's taken me years to develop this richly flavoured stock recipe, which is why the measurements for the vegetables are so precise (of course you can vary them slightly if you wish). If you prefer a lighter fish stock, double the amount of water.

Makes 600 ml
750 g snapper carcasses, or whole snapper, chopped into large chunks
⅓ cup extra-virgin olive oil
150 g brown onion, sliced
150 g carrot, sliced
50 g celery, sliced
75 g fennel, sliced (optional)
75 g mushrooms, sliced (optional)
3 cloves garlic, sliced
15 g ginger, sliced
5 strips orange peel
6 sprigs flat-leaf parsley
6 sprigs thyme
2 dried bay leaves
½ cup white wine
1½ cups water

Wash snapper carcasses or whole snapper well to remove any blood. Heat olive oil in a stockpot and cook onion, carrot, celery, fennel and mushrooms (if using) until soft but not browned. Add the fish bones, garlic, ginger, orange peel, parsley, thyme and bay leaves, and cook over a medium heat for a couple more minutes. Add wine and bring to the boil. Add water and return to the boil. Reduce heat, cover and simmer for 20–30 minutes. Strain.

Chicken stock
Makes about 2 litres
2 kg chicken carcasses, crushed
200 g carrots, finely chopped
1 leek, sliced
1 medium brown onion, chopped
1 small stick celery, sliced
2 cloves garlic, sliced
½ cup white wine
2 litres cold water
1 dried bay leaf
few sprigs flat-leaf parsley
few sprigs thyme

Combine all ingredients except water in a large saucepan and heat until wine boils. Add water, return to the boil, reduce heat

and simmer for 3 hours, skimming frequently. This recipe can also be used to make game stock from game trimmings.

Veal stock
Makes about 1.5 litres
2.5 kg veal shanks (meat and bones), cut into pieces
500 g pig's trotters
250 g carrots, chopped
150 g onions, chopped
50 g celery, chopped
¼ head garlic
3 dried bay leaves
few sprigs flat-leaf parsley
few sprigs thyme

Cover shanks and trotters with cold water in a large saucepan and bring to a simmer. Gently stir to loosen any impurities and skim the surface carefully. Add remaining ingredients and bring to the boil, then cover, reduce heat to very low and simmer for 10–12 hours (many would cook it for less, but I find it takes 10–12 hours for all the gelatine to be released) adding more water as necessary. Strain through a fine sieve, squeezing the solids to extract as much flavour as possible. Discard solids and pass liquid through a muslin cloth. You can freeze stock, or reduce it to the veal glaze below then freeze it in ice-cube trays. When you need 1 cup stock, place 1 large or 2 small ice-cubes into a measuring cup, fill it with hot water and stir to dissolve; add more cubes of stock if you prefer a stronger flavour. If pork is not to your taste, you can substitute 500 g chicken feet for the pig's trotters.

Veal glaze
Boil Veal Stock (see above) until reduced to ½ litre. Glaze can be frozen in ice-cube trays and added to soups and stews; 1 large ice cube diluted in 1 cup water will give you a real broth. After cooking a steak in a pan, deglaze the pan with some red wine, an ice-cube of veal glaze and a little butter, for a wonderful sauce. Veal stock and veal glaze are available at good butchers if you don't have time to make your own.

Vegetable stock (court bouillon)

Makes about 2 litres

2 litres water
2 cups white wine
2 large carrots, chopped
2 large brown onions, chopped
1 stick celery, chopped
6 dried bay leaves
8 cloves garlic, chopped
4 sprigs thyme
1 bulb fennel, sliced
1 teaspoon white peppercorns

Place all ingredients in a large saucepan, bring to the boil and simmer for 30 minutes. Strain, cool and refrigerate.

Handmade Sicilian-style macaroni

You'll need a clean metal knitting needle (or I usually cut a 30 cm strip from a wire coat hanger) to roll the macaroni around. It's important to measure the ingredients accurately – if the dough is too wet it will stick to the needle, and if it's too dry it won't roll around it. This can be quite a fun thing to make with a few friends.

Serves 6 as a main course or 12 as a side dish

500 g plain flour
1 teaspoon salt
1 × 60 g egg
150 ml water

Mix flour, salt, egg and water in an electric mixer and knead, using a dough hook or by hand, for 3–5 minutes, until dough comes together and is very smooth. It needs to be quite dry. Wrap in plastic film and rest in the refrigerator for 5–6 hours or overnight. Break off a piece of dough the size of a small walnut. Roll it around the knitting needle then roll between the palm of your hand and a clean, dry work surface until it is about 20 cm long. Gently slide tube off the knitting needle and set aside on a clean, dry tea towel for 1 hour to dry. Repeat with remaining dough. Bring a large pot of salted water to the boil and cook macaroni for about 5 minutes.

Greek filo pastry

125 g plain flour
¼ teaspoon salt
¼ cup water (approximately)

Combine the flour, salt and water into a dough. Knead until smooth then wrap in plastic film and leave to rest at room temperature for 1 hour. Cut dough in half. It should be soft, to ensure the filo will be very thin. Using plenty of extra flour to avoid sticking, roll dough through the machine repeatedly, each time reducing the setting by one notch, until you reach the thinnest setting, and then roll at least 3 times until pastry is paper-thin. If it gets too long to handle at any stage, cut it into manageable pieces. Now you can stretch it gently with your hands if you want to make it even thinner. When working with filo pastry, keep it covered with plastic film to prevent it drying out. Pastry kept in the fridge will discolour after 1 day, but it will keep well in the freezer for a couple of months if wrapped in plastic film.

Ras el hanout

It's best to grind your own spices fresh from whole spices, but I've also given ground measurements below. Ras El Hanout (meaning 'top of the shop') comes in many different combinations, and is used in many North African-influenced dishes. It is available in specialist spice shops.

Makes 3½ tablespoons

1 tablespoon green cardamom pods (3 teaspoons ground)
1 large cinnamon stick (3 teaspoons ground)
1 small nutmeg (1½ teaspoons ground)
1 teaspoon cloves (¾ teaspoon ground)
2 teaspoons white peppercorns (3 teaspoons ground)
2 teaspoons black peppercorns (3 teaspoons ground)
1 teaspoon ground cayenne pepper

Remove seeds from cardamom pods. Crumble cinnamon sticks. Chop nutmeg into small pieces. Combine all spices and grind using a mortar and pestle or a spice and coffee grinder. Pass through a fine sieve and regrind anything that's left behind. Store in an airtight container in a cool, dark cupboard.

Quatre épices (Four spices)

This classic spice blend is one of the main seasonings in French charcuterie. It can also be purchased as a readymade blend.

Makes about ¾ cup
70 g black peppercorns, ground
10 g cloves, ground
10 g freshly grated nutmeg
10 g cinnamon, ground

Combine all spices. Store in an airtight container in a cool, dry place.

Dijon mustard vinaigrette

This is a good vinaigrette for dressing coarse, bitter leaves, such as radicchio.

Makes 160 ml
¼ teaspoon salt
15 ml white wine vinegar
¼ teaspoon freshly ground white pepper
1 tablespoon Dijon mustard
120 ml extra-virgin olive oil

Dissolve salt in the vinegar and mix in pepper. Add mustard and olive oil and whisk to combine. Mustard vinaigrette will keep longer than plain vinaigrette, as the mustard acts as a preservative. It will keep for up to 1 month in an airtight container in the fridge.

Saffron potatoes
Makes 6 generous serves
½ cup olive oil
8 cloves garlic, chopped
½ teaspoon saffron threads
2 cups Chicken, Fish or Vegetable Stock (see above)
1 cup water
1 kg small kipfler potatoes, peeled and cut into thick slices
salt, to taste

Heat oil and fry garlic until lightly browned. Add saffron, stock, water and potatoes, bring to the boil, reduce heat to very low and simmer for about 20 minutes, until a skewer just comes out of potatoes easily. Add salt just before potatoes have finished cooking. Serve immediately or refrigerate with remaining liquid for 1–2 days; gently reheat in this liquid when required.

Roast tomato sauce

Make this very simple sauce in the middle of summer, when tomatoes are at their peak. In winter, it's better to use good Italian tinned tomatoes, rather than tasteless, under-ripe fresh ones. I always roast tomatoes when making a tomato sauce, in order to get the most flavour. This sauce is perfect as is over pasta.

Makes 1 cup
500 g ripe tomatoes
¼ cup extra-virgin olive oil
salt, to taste
freshly ground black pepper, to taste

Preheat oven to 175°C. Cut tomatoes in half, place on a baking tray, drizzle with olive oil and sprinkle with salt and pepper. Roast until soft, about 1 hour. Push through a sieve, with all of the cooking juices, to make a thick purée. The sauce will keep for 4–5 days in the fridge or for 3 months in the freezer.

Preserved lemons

This recipe is an ideal use for bush lemons, since their skin is less bitter than that of conventional lemons. I use Preserved Lemons in many ways – cut into salads, grilled and served with meats and fish, and, of course, when cooking lamb.

6 lemons or bush lemons (when available)
3 tablespoons salt
3 dried bay leaves, crumbled
6 sprigs thyme
extra-virgin olive oil, to cover

Place lemons in a saucepan, cover with boiling water, place a weight on top to submerge the lemons and leave overnight. Next day, drain lemons and cover with cold water. Set aside for 2 days, changing the water 4 times a day.

Cut lemons into very thin slices, discarding the ends. Sprinkle with salt and refrigerate, covered, for a day, turning once. Next day, place lemons and the salty liquid in a couple of jars with bay leaves, thyme and enough olive oil to cover. (Using a couple of jars rather than one will ensure that the oil coats all slices.) Refrigerate for at least a week before using.

Sugar syrup
Makes about 1.6 litres
1 kg sugar
1 litre water

Combine sugar and water and bring to the boil, then remove from heat immediately. Sugar Syrup keeps almost indefinitely in the fridge.

Hazelnut praline
1 cup hazelnuts
1 cup sugar
½ cup water

Preheat oven to 150°C. Toast hazelnuts in the oven (150°C) for about 20 minutes until skin darkens a little. Wrap in a tea towel while still hot and rub well to remove most of the skin. Combine sugar and water in a saucepan and boil over a high heat until it has a light caramel colour, add nuts and pour onto a lightly oiled baking tray. Leave at room temperature until cold. Tip onto a chopping board, cover with a couple of layers of plastic film and hit gently with a meat mallet until crumbed. Place in an airtight container and keep for a few days or freeze until needed.

Almond praline
Plunge 1 cup almonds into boiling water for 30 seconds, then drain and rinse under cold water. Squeeze almonds out of their skins, then toast on a baking tray in the oven (150°C) for about 20 minutes, or until golden. Proceed as for Hazelnut Praline.

Pastry cream
3 eggs yolks
⅓ cup castor sugar
¼ cup plain flour
1 cup milk
½ small vanilla bean, split
¾ cup 45%-fat cream, whipped

Whisk yolks with half the sugar until pale. Sift flour over the egg mixture and mix well. Combine milk, vanilla bean and remaining sugar in a saucepan and bring to the boil. Pour hot milk into the egg mixture, whisking constantly. Return mixture to the saucepan and stir over a low heat until it just comes to a simmer. Reduce heat to very low and continue stirring for 4–5 minutes. Remove from heat and stir for 1 minute. Push through a fine sieve into a bowl. Scrape vanilla seeds from bean and stir them through the Pastry Cream. Cover with plastic film, gently pressing the film onto the surface of the custard, to prevent a skin forming. Refrigerate. Just before serving, remove pastry cream from fridge, beat well with a wooden spoon to loosen, then fold through whipped cream. For extra flavour, you can stir through ¾ cup Hazelnut or Almond Praline (see above), or finely chopped candied peel, just before using.

Index

LANTERN

Published by the Penguin Group
Penguin Group (Australia)
250 Camberwell Road, Camberwell, Victoria 3124, Australia
(a division of Pearson Australia Group Pty Ltd)
Penguin Group (USA) Inc.
375 Hudson Street, New York, New York 10014, USA
Penguin Group (Canada)
90 Eglinton Avenue East, Suite 700, Toronto ON M4P 2Y3, Canada
(a division of Pearson Penguin Canada Inc.)
Penguin Books Ltd
80 Strand, London WC2R 0RL, England
Penguin Ireland
25 St Stephen's Green, Dublin 2, Ireland
(a division of Penguin Books Ltd)
Penguin Books India Pvt Ltd
11 Community Centre, Panchsheel Park, New Delhi – 110 017, India
Penguin Group (NZ)
Cnr Airborne and Rosedale Roads, Albany, Auckland, New Zealand
(a division of Pearson New Zealand Ltd)
Penguin Books (South Africa) (Pty) Ltd
24 Sturdee Avenue, Rosebank, Johannesburg 2196, South Africa

Penguin Books Ltd, Registered Offices: 80 Strand, London WC2R 0RL, England

First published by Penguin Group (Australia), a division of Pearson Australia Group Pty Ltd, 2006

10 9 8 7 6 5 4 3 2 1

Text copyright © Janni Kyritsis 2006
Photographs copyright © Ian Wallace 2006

Design by John Canty © Penguin Group (Australia)
Cover and author photographs by Ian Wallace
Styling by David Morgan
Text written with the assistance of Roberta Muir
Typeset in Stempel Garamond and Univers by Post Pre-press Group, Brisbane, Queensland
Colour reproduction by Splitting Image, Clayton, Victoria
Printed and bound in Singapore by Imago Productions

National Library of Australia
Cataloguing-in-Publication data:

    Kyritsis, Janni.
    Wild weed pie.

    Includes index.
    ISBN-13: 978 1 92098 932 3.
    ISBN-10: 1 920989 32 3.

    1. Cookery. I. Wallace, Ian, 1959–. II. Title.

    641.5

www.penguin.com.au

Acknowledgements

Restaurants would not exist without their dedicated
staff, and for that I would like to thank all the people
who worked with me at MG Garage and Fuel. I'd also
like to thank my friends for their help and support
throughout my career, and the team who put this
book together: Julie Gibbs, Nicola Young, John Canty,
Ian Wallace and David Morgan. Thanks also to Mitch,
for assistance with some of the recipe testing.

Thanks are due to the following outlets for their
generous assistance with props.

Accoutrement (02 9969 1031)
The Art of Wine and Food (02 9363 2817)
Bisanna Tiles (02 9310 2500)
Bodum (02 9389 1488)
Camargue (02 9960 6234)
The Ceramic Shed (02 4627 9651)
Chee Soon and Fitzgerald (02 9360 1031)
Country Road (1800 801 911)
Major & Tom (02 9557 8380)
Mud Australia (02 9300 8377)
91 Bourke Street (02 8356 9401)
Orson & Blake (02 9326 1155)
Papaya (02 9386 9980)
Simon Johnson (02 9328 6888)
Tiletecnics (02 8399 1288)
Wheel&Barrow (02 9389 9022)
Your Display Gallery (02 9906 7556)